decorating easy

DECORATING
easy

Create a simple,
comfortable home with
pure style

Jane Cumberbatch

QUADRILLE

SPECIAL PHOTOGRAPHY BY JENNY ZARINS

ILLUSTRATIONS BY KATE STORER

*For Alastair, Tom,
Georgie, and Gracie*

Editorial Director Jane O'Shea
Creative Director Helen Lewis
Project Editor Lisa Pendreigh
Designer Lawrence Morton
Photographer Jenny Zarins
Illustrator Kate Storer
Styling Assistant Charlotte Kennedy-Cochran-Patrick
Production Director Vincent Smith
Production Controller Ruth Deary

This edition published in 2006 by Quadrille Publishing Ltd.,
Alhambra House, 27–31 Charing Cross Road, London WC2H OLS

Text and project design © Jane Cumberbatch 2005
Photography, illustrations, design, and layout ©
Quadrille Publishing Ltd. 2005

Cataloguing in Publication Data: a record of this book is
available from the British Library.

ISBN-13: 978 184400 423 2
ISBN-10: 1 84400 423 6

Printed in Singapore

contents

PART 1

Pearls of wisdom

down to earth

USE SIMPLE IDEAS AND FLEXIBLE THINKING TO MAKE YOUR HOME A HAVEN FROM THE STRESSES AND STRAINS OF DAILY LIFE.

Decorating Easy is about making your home comfortable and modern without spending a fortune. My ideas will, hopefully, enable you to create a stylish space on a budget, without forsaking looks and function. *Decorating Easy* is not about having a glossy show house; increasingly, the home has become the ultimate trophy, something to show off, rather than a domestic necessity. It is rather more down to earth (more earthy than earnest) and more in tune with real life and its imperfections than the ultra-perfect interiors that advertisers seduce us into believing we should aspire to.

Decorating Easy is making the best of what you've got, and thinking in a more resourceful, and, wherever possible, a more eco-conscious way. It is about paring down and living with less to keep your life more in control. And it is also about learning to be elastic in your planning and thinking, so your aims and needs are more likely to be realized.

decorating easy means:

* writing down your list of priorities: getting the big jobs, such as electrics and plumbing, done first

* doing as much as you can yourself

* reviving a tired interior with fresh coats of your favorite paint

* not hankering after the last word in kitchen design, trendy sofas, and so on (otherwise your budget will soon become a teeny-weeny one); basic designs can look just as good

* shopping in ordinary stores for cheap, functional, but good-looking objects: candles, bowls, good brooms, and so on

* waiting for the sales to chase bargains in linen sheets, cashmere throws, good saucepans, and other "investment" life-nourishing luxuries

* getting two or three rooms in shape to reflect your style and make you feel at home until you have the funds to do up the rest

* paring down and making a decisive style statement: get rid of anything that clashes with your aesthetic—sell it or take it to a thrift shop

* updating everything from a junk table with a lick of paint to an sagging armchair with a fresh new flowery slipcover

* living with less, but carefully selecting the objects you derive most pleasure from

Flower power

Flowers give a space immediate life, color, and scent. I usually put all of one type in a vase or tank, but mixed bunches of garden roses, lime green alchemilla, summer buds, and herbs look very pretty and informal. And I also like to mix big, blowsy blooms, such as roses and peonies, in simple metal buckets on the table for an outdoor summer feast. Here are some notes on my favorite flowers:

Spring   wallflowers, feathery parrot tulips, daffodils, white narcissi, pussy willow, sticky bud branches

Summer   alliums, cut herbs, garden roses ('Constance Spry,' 'Gertrude Jekyll,' 'John Clare'), rosemary, lavender, peonies, agapanthus, nasturtiums, cornflowers, sunflowers

Fall   zinnias, flowering cabbages, anemones, hydrangeas

Winter   forced bulbs for color and scent in baskets and pots with moss for bedding: narcissi, hyacinths, amaryllis, greenery from the garden to weave into a simple Christmas wreath for the door

making your home human

DON'T AIM FOR PERFECTION. WITH THE EMPHASIS SOLELY ON LOOKS, MANY INTERIOR STYLE BIBLES MISS THE NOTION THAT HOME SHOULD BE AN OASIS OF COMFORT.

Don't be too precious

Be easy on yourself—your home should be relaxed and welcoming, not uptight and squeaky clean. It may be hip to have a sleek East-meets-West white and taupe linen look, but what a nuisance if you spill the take-out curry, or your children make a nest for their rabbit on the dry-clean-only sofa. Although it would be delicious to slip between freshly laundered linen sheets every day, it actually doesn't matter if you don't have the energy to run an iron over the bedclothes, polish the table until it shines, or make the bed with surgical precision.

Buy tough, washable fabrics, like canvas and cotton ticking, that can be thrown in the washing machine. I have white cotton slipcovers that are a magnet for muddy paw prints but one hot wash cycle swiftly deals with them, and they come out as good as new. Likewise, choose wall paints that are easy to wipe down. And if you try to live with less, it's easier to keep your home looking reasonably clean and neat.

Let in light, and keep in warmth

Let daylight flood your home to give it a fresh, airy feel; cleaning the windows is one job that is worth doing regularly.

Pools of soft light, whether from lamps or lighted candles, are soothing at nighttime and can make everyday eating a sensual experience. Never use harsh overhead lighting.

In winter, keep your nest warm and cozy with proper insulation, efficient heating (infloor is ideal), and, most comforting of all, a roaring wood fire.

Go for what feels good

Natural textures look and feel more comfortable than most synthetics. Opt for soft wool blankets; thick, fluffy cotton towels; and crisp cotton sheets. Try to avoid the shine factor: satin sheets are too tarty. Likewise, nylon sheets are too "trailer park", and they give you electric shocks.

Similarly, surfaces that are easy to maintain and robust are more pleasing to live with—such as wooden countertops, waxed wood floors, smooth stainless steel kitchen accessories, and flat, matte-painted finishes.

Upholstery should be robust, while yielding just enough so you can sink back and relax among soft, voluptuous cushions.

Smell sweet

Smell affects our evaluation of things so much so that if you give someone two cans of identical furniture polish, one of which has a pleasant aroma, they will swear that the scented one works better. Thus, manufacturers are obsessed with chemically scenting their wares—and boy, do they smell noxious—from the detergents that claim to make our underwear smell "tropical" to "fresh from the fields" air fresheners. Throw them out—be eco and take them to the dump—and fill your home with the natural sensory pleasures of a freshly baked cake, hot buttered toast, and a freshly beeswaxed floor, or good scented candle, with real floral essences: all honest smells that make our homes desirable places to be.

building your nest

ELASTIC THINKING WILL EASE THE PROCESS OF PLANNING AND REALIZING YOUR DREAMS FOR A SNUG AND PRACTICAL HOME.

Find somewhere to roost

If an area is fashionable, house prices will be inflated, so it makes some sense to go to the most uncool spot you can find. Many people chant the mantra "location, location, location"; but for me, having swapped a hip-and-happening city pad for a large suburban house with dozens of rooms and a great garden, there is more to life than living where it's supposedly all "at."

Once you have decided on the area you wish to target, drive around and view as many properties as possible to get an idea of what you want and what your money will buy. Even if a house or apartment isn't obviously for sale or rent, put a note through the mail slot stating your intentions. This is a very good way of avoiding realtors and their charges.

Be flexible

You may have set your heart on a charming old farmhouse; but if it needs massive restoration, you might find it more expedient to consider something different, like a well-built sixties property, which will probably be in better condition and more light filled. With the money saved, you could also add an outbuilding, such as a home office or an adults-only retreat. Look for a home with sound "bones". Beware of flimsy structures where soundproofing might be negligible, insulation lacking, and the finishing third-rate.

When you find a property that you like, return several times to view it at different times of the day, in order to see how the light changes, if a quiet road assumes an expressway character at rush hour, or whether the next-door neighbors are all-night party groovers.

Be prepared

The uncertainties of house prices and the high cost of moving may lead you to stay put and improve your existing environment. I suggest that you tackle major jobs, like the kitchen, bathroom and heating system to enjoy now; such improvements can also add value later. The idea of a pricey sunroom might be wonderful, but it's unlikely that you'll recoup the cost when you decide to move.

Hired help

Tackle simple jobs yourself—like painting, shelving, and assembling prefabricated furniture. Equipment suppliers give out extensive leaflets on how to do most jobs, so decide what you might attempt yourself and what is best left to experts, such as plumbing, wiring, gas repairs, or removing hazardous materials like asbestos.

Hiring laborers for building and decorating work is where you can lose control and cash, unless you are specific in communicating your needs. This means writing everything down to make sure there are no gray areas and keeping a close eye on what's being done.

The best way to find a building contractor is by word of mouth: go to see any previous work that he and his team have done, and ask the client whether they finished on time and within budget. Get several estimates before you agree a price, and pay in stages, never upfront. Get the contractor to agree to a schedule in writing, but be prepared for those eventualities that are out of everyone's hands, such as bad weather, unexpected rot, or delays with materials. Allow an extra 10 percent on top of your budget as a safety net.

If you appear to be on the case (don't go on vacation the day they start) and are polite (it's tough putting up with strangers making a mess in your home, but they are doing a job), you are more likely to get the job done to your satisfaction and on time. Building contractors pet hates are histrionics and changes of mind.

Golden rules

* Plan ahead any outside jobs, such as roofing, pointing, and exterior painting, that are best done during the summer months. The optimum time for any garden work is during spring, when the ground is neither too dry nor frozen.

* Wear old clothes, or invest in a pair of painters' overalls.

* When painting and sanding, cover floors and furniture with drop cloths.

* When painting, mask off any areas that you want to avoid with low-tack tape.

* If the kitchen is out of action, rig up a temporary one with a camping stove and microwave. Try to ensure that you have some access to water.

* Stock up on coffee and/or tea for the builders. It helps to make them feel loved, so they will be more likely to do a better job.

* Don't let the builders get at your vacuum cleaner; plaster dust and sawdust spell death to the domestic vacuum. Rent an industrial one if they don't bring their own.

* Look up the address of your local dump and dumpster rental company, as garbage collectors will not usually take away half-finished paint cans or building rubble. Dumpsters usually need licenses, so apply to your local authority.

creating a mood board

GIVE IDEAS FOCUS WITH A MOOD BOARD, USING SAMPLES OF COLORS AND FABRICS. BUY A THICK PIECE OF WHITE POSTER BOARD—NO MORE THAN A YARD SQUARE—AND SECURE SWATCHES TO IT WITH THUMBTACKS, MASKING TAPE, OR SPRAY ADHESIVE.

Fabrics Use vibrant fabrics as accent colors against a canvas of white, lavender, or gray. I have a passion for fuchsia pink cotton velvet, pink muslin, and lime green checks, which I make into simple cushions and shades.

1. **Creamy unbleached muslin** A utilitarian fabric available in various weights. Use the heaviest for chair covers and cushions. Buy from yard goods departments or, for larger quantities, wholesalers. Preshrink before use.

2. **Gingham** Basic, but sweet. Looks good as chair covers, cushions, simple curtains, and decorated lamps. Gingham looks really groovy when used in a "domestic goddess" apron (see pages 130–31).

3. **Tana cotton lawn** I can't think of anything better than Liberty floral prints, which come in such beautiful colors and patterns. Not cheap, but Tana Lawn is very tough and can be made into cushions and floaty curtains.

4. **Polka-dot cotton** Retro dots are everywhere and, like checks, plaids, and stripes, have a utilitarian appeal. Use for pretty cushions (see pages 140–41), aprons, linings for laundry bags and for summer ideas like a "teeny-weeny polka-dot bikini."

5. **Striped cotton ticking** I choose bold blue-and-white stripes for outdoors—chaises, awnings, windbreaks—and more subtle woven ticking, which looks simple yet contemporary, made into curtains (see pages 146–7) and chair covers.

Trims and ties, ribbons and bows I collect lengths of ribbon and rick-rack to use as edgings on cushions, lampshades, and sheets and to make pretty ties for pillowcases, bags, and other accessories.

Wallpaper Bold geometric and floral prints make a more decisive statement than less exuberant patterns and work well along just one wall, a good budget option. One of my favorite looks is a country garden flower print (see pages 44–5 and 68–9).

Paint Flat and eggshell finishes look more natural than gloss ones and have an appealing opaque effect. Around the house, pure white paint is really adaptable—wraparound white can update a tired interior for not much financial outlay.

To give a room a calm and natural background color, I like to use mint greens, pale lavenders, and soft country creams, which allow me to punctuate with splashes of bright color in cushions, flowers, and other details.

For the most part—subtropical zones and hot climates excepted—hot pinks, blues, oranges, and other strong colors need to be used with caution to avoid color overkill. Having said this, it's great to liven up a piece of furniture with cornflower blue painted detail (see pages 136–7) or to make a workspace sing with great pink and white painted stripes (see pages 118–19). The secret is to use clear, bright colors and to avoid the kind of harsh colors that mass manufacturers use for everything from cars to cooking pots.

hot pink

lavender

gingham checks and polka dots

floral cotton lawn

strawberry pink

country florals

pale blue

sludgy blue

cornflower

bean green

soft green

mint green

chalk white

blue and white stripes

ribbons and rickrack

planning and sketching

PUT YOUR DECORATING IDEAS DOWN ON PAPER. DRAW A BASIC ROOM PLAN TO GET AN IDEA OF WHERE EVERYTHING MIGHT GO AND A SIMPLE SKETCH TO GET A FEEL FOR THE COLORS AND FABRICS YOU WANT TO USE.

A plan drawn on graph or quadrille paper allows you to accurately map out where all the services, such as electrical outlets and plumbing, will be and whether everything fits into the space. Don't worry too much about your drawing skills (I suggest working in pencil if you're unsure—mistakes can be rubbed out—and coloring in with watercolor or colored pencil). If necessary, the final versions can be finished with thin pen lines for extra definition.

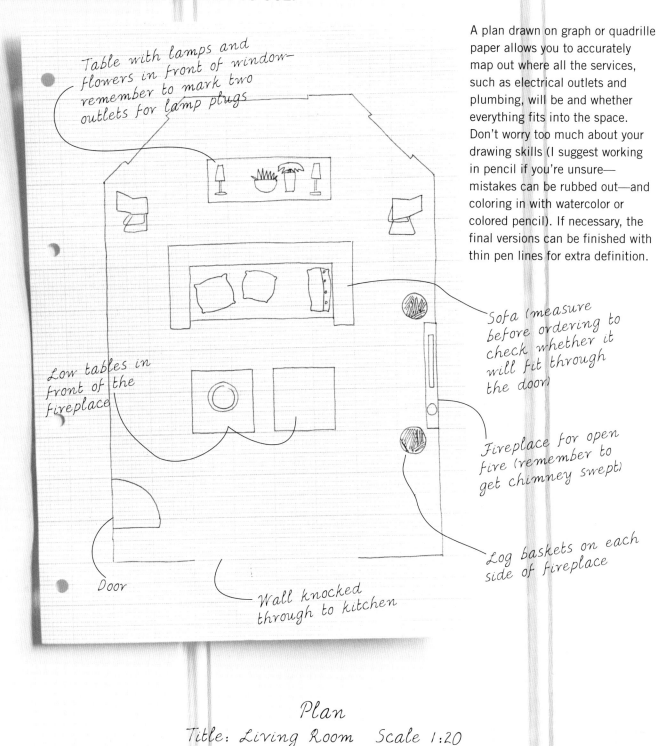

Table with lamps and flowers in front of window—remember to mark two outlets for lamp plugs

Low tables in front of the fireplace

Door

Wall knocked through to kitchen

Sofa (measure before ordering to check whether it will fit through the door)

Fireplace for open fire (remember to get chimney swept)

Log baskets on each side of fireplace

Plan
Title: Living Room   Scale 1:20

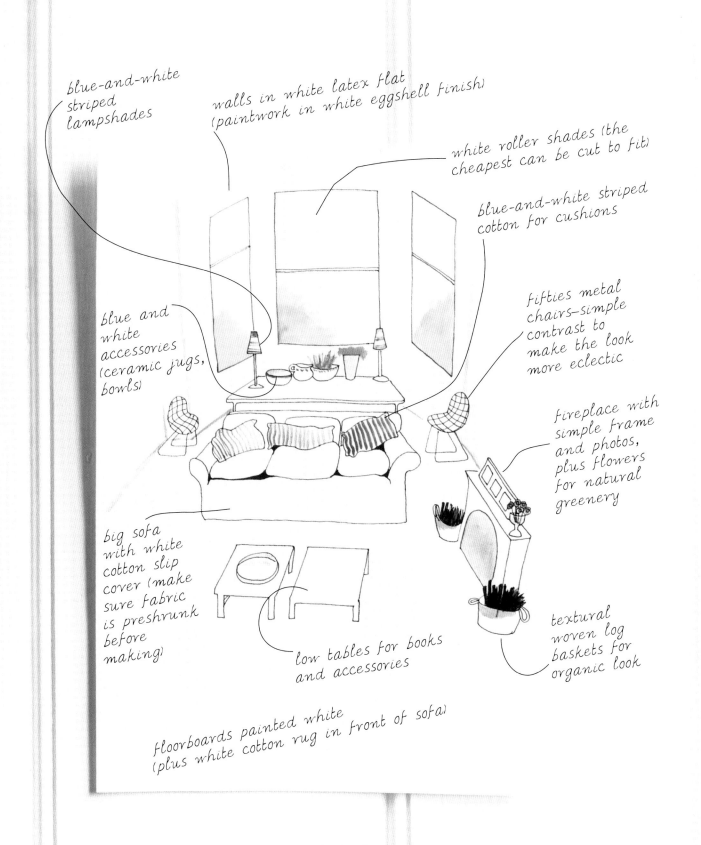

blue-and-white striped lampshades

walls in white latex flat (paintwork in white eggshell finish)

white roller shades (the cheapest can be cut to fit)

blue-and-white striped cotton for cushions

fifties metal chairs—simple contrast to make the look more eclectic

blue and white accessories (ceramic jugs, bowls)

fireplace with simple frame and photos, plus flowers for natural greenery

big sofa with white cotton slip cover (make sure fabric is preshrunk before making)

low tables for books and accessories

textural woven log baskets for organic look

floorboards painted white (plus white cotton rug in front of sofa)

Sketch

A simple plan: blue and white living room—fresh, modern, and airy

top 10 decorating tools

HAVING A BASIC TOOL KIT IS THE ONLY WAY TO PRACTISE HOME D.I.Y.; WITHOUT IT, NO JOB CAN BE COMPLETED EFFICIENTLY. I KNOW THAT EVERY SELF-RESPECTING BUILDER OR D.I.Y. ENTHUSIAST WILL OWN A FAR GRANDER AND MORE EXTENSIVE BATTERY OF USEFUL GADGETS, BUT HERE ARE TEN ITEMS THAT I MUST HAVE ON HAND BEFORE I TACKLE THE MOST FREQUENTLY EXECUTED DECORATING JOBS.

1 tool box
You need somewhere to put all your tools; otherwise a state of disorganization occurs. I use a simple plastic box with a click lid that opens up to reveal a removable top shelf, with compartments for storing nails, screws, and anchors, and space below for bigger items, like claw hammers and screwdrivers.

2 sharp scissors
For cutting everything from wallpaper to string.

3 extending tape measure
A 25-ft. (7.6m) length is best for measuring jobs.

4 mineral spirits/turpentine
Absolutely essential for cleaning oil-based paints off brushes (water is fine for latex paint).

5 paintbrushes
A set of four will cope with most jobs: 4-in. (100mm) brush for latex, 2-in. (50mm) and 1-in. (25mm) for oil-based paint, and $\frac{1}{2}$-in. (12mm) cutting-in brush for window frames and straight lines.

6 paint roller
Quicker than a brush for applying latex paint to walls and ceilings. Sponge rollers are cheaper, but spatter paint; lambswool and mohair best.

7 spirit level
For keeping all straight lines straight.

8 sandpaper
In different grades. Also a block of wood to wrap paper around for smoothing or roughening surfaces.

9 pencil
An HB or a 2 is best for marking measurements on walls and other surfaces.

10 filler
Makes even the most ravaged and pitted walls presentable. Use all-purpose for wood and plaster.

Start with my top ten decorating tools, then add to your tool kit as your needs grow. Always buy the best you can afford. There are some useful pieces of kit that you will use quite often. Rent any expensive items, such as a steamer for stripping wallpaper, that will rarely be needed.

- ✓ Two-speed electric drill plus a range of bits
- ✓ Claw hammer
- ✓ Tenon saw and hacksaw
- ✓ Single-slot and Phillips screwdrivers
- ✓ Steel rule
- ✓ Bradawl
- ✓ Chisel
- ✓ Adjustable wrench
- ✓ Cutting knife
- ✓ Goggles and heavy-duty gloves

decorating clinic

HERE ARE MY ANSWERS TO SOME COMMON DECORATING DILEMMAS.

Q: What will the neighbors think? I don't like curtains and want as much light as possible to flood in through my windows, but can I leave them bare?

A: Even if nosy neighbors are not your concern, you must surely agree that a degree of modesty is required in the bathroom. A simple roller shade in white cotton or even a panel of stretched muslin will provide a screen but at the same time filter the light. Alternatively, consider fitting opaque glass.

Q: Can I decorate with pink, or is it strictly for sissies?

A: I thoroughly recommend it. Although shocking pink is my favorite pink for lipstick, I would stop short at washing my walls all over in such a loud shade. Why not paint a wall in strawberry pink ice-cream-colored stripes—a groovy choice, even for a teenage boy (see pages 118–19).

Q: My bedroom is tiny. How can I make it look bigger?

A: You can't go wrong with wraparound white to create an illusion of space. Get clutter out of sight. If it won't all fit in your closet, put some under the bed or in a simple cabinet, painted white. Be ruthless in removing excess clutter, and have only what you need and use regularly.

Q: How cool is it to color coordinate?

A: Like dressing from head-to-toe in black, as urban creative types are prone to, plunging a room into monotone is frankly very dull. Unless you want an impersonal hotel lobby look, I suggest you play with color and have fun with it. I am particularly fond of plain white backgrounds, against which I put shots of bright color—pink or mint green, for example—in furniture and objects.

Q: How do I please a demanding teenage daughter?

A: Make her feel like a princess with one of those floaty mosquito net devices (see pages 72–3) and some great colored bed linens. Let her flood the room with pink light, even if it makes the room look like a brothel; burn evil-smelling joss sticks; play loud rock music (between 8:00 P.M. and 9:00 P.M. only); and cover her walls with as many teeny boy band pin-ups as she desires. At least there will be fewer issues to argue about.

Q: I've spent months trying to find the perfect white. I'm down to a shortlist of fifty, so what do I do next?

A: Life's too short to fret over such details, unless you're rich enough to employ someone to do the choosing for you. Remember that a paint sample takes on a different color when it's transposed to a whole room, and can therefore lead you into more agonizing. I suggest you go straight to your favorite hardware store and ask for their best brilliant white latex flat. Trust me, it will look fab!

Q: Art. Yes or no?

A: If there's nothing that you desire to see every minute of the day, then leave your walls bare. There's no need to have pictures on the wall just because you feel you ought to and the Have-Everythings down the road do. I am very keen on black-and-white family photos (see pages 138–9).

Q: I'm stuck with old-fashioned radiators. How can I make them less obtrusive?

A: Live with them, but help them melt into the background by painting them the same color as the walls. There are now some very good radiator paints on the market.

Q: It's going to cost squillions to carpet my stairs. Any tips?

A: Have you thought about painting them instead? It is much cheaper and really stylish, but you will have to educate the family in negotiating them using fairy-like steps (see pages 28–9).

Q: What about beige?

A: Too safe and too dull. Avoid it at all costs. I once interviewed the late society decorator David Hicks, who said it was the color his clients demanded most, so it only goes to show that cash doesn't equal decorating sense. Beige-like colors should be allowed only in items that are naturally beige, such as soft wool blankets and woven baskets.

Q: I'm moving out of the city but don't want to abandon all my urban sensibilities. Can I do country-style without the chintz?

A: Absolutely, so long as you stay clear of kitchen airers festooned with dried flowers and herbs, and shelves groaning with blue and white china.

Q: What's the cheapest way to store kitchen plates and other dishes?

A: Keep control of your mind and life with simple open shelves for all your kitchen goods. Home centers usually have lengths of wood and simple brackets. Alternatively, you could recycle old shelving that you might have somewhere else in the house.

Q: What can I do with the perfectly hideous dining table and chairs that my mother-in-law gave us? My husband won't part with it.

A: He probably doesn't like it either but feels duty bound to keep it. Proceed with cunning and advertise it on eBay. If you get a good offer, dangle it in front of him: the lure of some "holding and folding" might just do the trick!

make and do

WITH THE SENSE OF COMFORT IT PROVIDES, DOMESTICITY IS EVER MORE APPEALING, IN OUR QUICK-FIX SOCIETY. MAKING SIMPLE THINGS FOR ONESELF GIVES THAT WARM FEELING OF WELL-BEING AND ACHIEVEMENT.

Just as baking a birthday cake and decorating it with rosettes and candles is so much more pleasurable than coming home with a perfectly formed, but not-half-as-tasty specimen from the store, so running up a pretty cushion or trimming a blanket is more satisfying, and individual, than what is available to buy in the stores.

You don't have to use up all your precious spare time slaving over a sewing machine. Specifically making the time to do a simple project is good for the soul and allows you to concentrate on something a little more creative than the latest soap opera. All the ideas in this book have simple instructions and are easy to follow and execute.

They will also help you to save money, as this book is about being resourceful and making the most of what you've got. For example, don't get rid of the paint dregs from a decorating job; there might be enough left over to renovate a junk table (see pages 124–5). Likewise, don't throw away old clothes; if they are in a great print, cut them up, and use the fabric for appliqué or a cushion cover or simple bag. Similarly, hunt in thrift shops, where you will certainly find some treasures, such as a perfectly good cream blanket that can be jazzed up with a velvet trim, or a tablecloth that can be dyed for a new look.

sewing essentials

* Sewing machine—buy a basic model if you're a beginner
* Fabric remnants—save any pieces left over from sewing jobs, and collect scraps from sales
* Trimmings—save any ribbons, rickrack, and bows from gifts
* Workbox—store everything in a plastic crate, or set aside a shelf or two in your work space. Use a separate bag for your remnants and trimmings
* Dressmaker's tape measure
* Ruler—for drawing straight lines
* Tailors' chalk—for marking fabric; use white for dark fabrics and colored for printed fabrics
* All-purpose scissors—for cutting out paper patterns
* Large dressmaking scissors—for cutting fabric
* Small embroidery scissors—for cutting threads
* Assorted sewing needles—for basting and other hand sewing
* Basting thread—easy to break when pulling out basting stitches. One type even dissolves with water or heat
* Seam ripper—a hooked device to help remove stitches
* Steam iron and ironing board
* Fabric dye—machine washable ones are best and can be used to dye both cottons and synthetics
* Elastic
* Touch-and-close tape—useful for closing cushion covers
* Buttons—a tin box of spare buttons is often useful
* Safety pins

key sewing tips

The secret of good sewing is a straight seam. Practice on small scraps of material to get going. Pinning and basting are key when stitching two or three pieces of fabric together, so they don't slip out of position when run through the machine. To make a plain seam, pin and baste the two layers together with right sides facing. Remove the pins and machine stitch. Remove the basting, and press the seam open.

There are various ways of finishing seams: fraying fabrics can be fixed by zigzag stitch, either before or after joining the seams, whereas non-fraying fabrics can be turned under and stitched.

To hem fabric, turn the hem to the wrong side to half the required depth, stitch, and press; turn hem over again, and pin or baste. Stitch close to the first fold. Press.

It's important to press as you go along to keep your sewing in shape and easy to handle. Use a steam iron or a damp cloth on the wrong side in order to prevent a shine on the fabric. Seams must be dampened before ironing so that they lie flat.

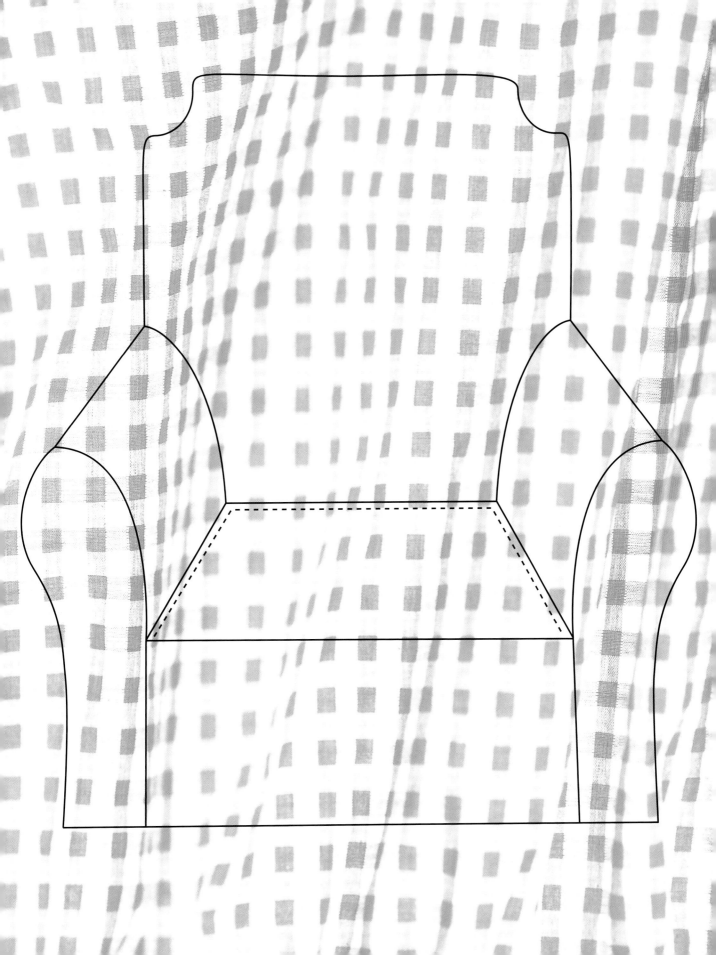

PART 2

Decorating secrets

step inside

10 WAYS TO MAKE A STYLISH ENTRANCE

1 Paint the front door in a fresh, light color—my favorite is egg blue—in tough exterior eggshell. No gloss paint, please.

2 Make sure that the front door is in keeping with the architectural style and period of the building.

3 Open up a dark hallway with layers of fresh white paint. If you prefer color, go for muted shades of blue, green, or lavender in small spaces. Larger spaces will not be overwhelmed by brighter shades, such as tulip pink or emerald green.

4 For a dramatic entrance, invest in a patterned wallpaper—a fabulous floral, geometric, or bold stripe, for example, looks good in cramped spaces. Wallpaper is not as economical as paint, but you can see exactly what you're getting.

5 To deal with muddy feet, lay down the thickest, scratchiest doormat you can find. Alternatively, fit some heavy-duty jute matting-like carpet, either as a doormat-sized piece by the door or in a length stretching down the hallway.

6 Think ergonomically. Position the hall light switch immediately to the right of the front door, so there's no fumbling in the dark. Install coat hooks to the left, preferably near a register, if you have these, to help dry wet coats.

7 Fill the biggest vase you have with some seasonal blooms—pussy willow in spring, a dewy bunch of garden roses in the summer, or a few dahlias in the fall.

8 Be completely ruthless, or at least try, and banish as much family clutter as you can. Install big baskets to store any stuff that gets dropped.

9 Hang a large mirror in the hallway to increase the sense of space and to check that you're looking pulled-together before dashing out of the house.

10 Make sure the lighting is welcoming. Try a pretty chandelier, a simple pendant shade, or a lamp on a side table. Recessed spotlights are also an option, but I think they look more hotel-like than home-sweet-home.

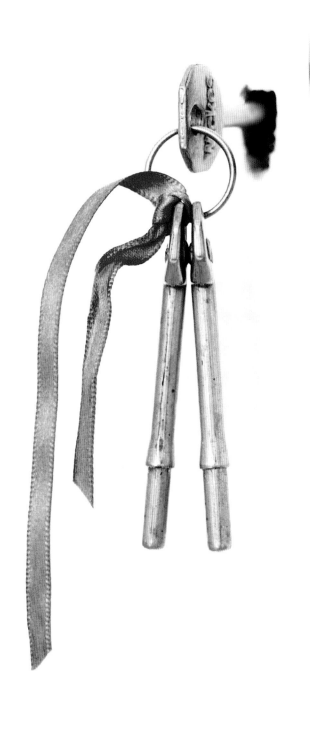

stellar stairway

CREATE A SENSE OF AIRY LIGHTNESS WITH A STAIRWAY PAINTED IN A FRESH WHITE COLOR SCHEME THAT IS HARDY ENOUGH TO WITHSTAND BUSY FAMILY TRAFFIC.

Provided noise is not an issue, there is absolutely nothing undressed about bare stairs, despite what your mother might say. When it comes to style, be firm; hold out for what you want, and, most importantly, don't threaten that not-inconsequential matter of the budget. Going back to—or rather up and down—the stair question, I think there is nothing simpler or more stylish than sanded and painted stairs, either fully painted or with a central strip left unpainted to look like a runner. Paint is much cheaper than a good carpet or sisal runner, which not only are costly but also need to be cut and fitted to size, an expense, as you'll need a professional to do it.

To achieve this look, pull on a pair of rubber gloves and thoroughly clean the stair treads with a bucket of hot water, detergent, and a good scrubbing brush. When the stairs are completely dry, measure the position of the runner in from both edges, and mark with two parallel strips of masking tape. Using a small paintbrush, apply a wood primer and undercoat, then finish off with two top coats of white floor paint. Don't use anything other than floor paint, as it will not be tough enough. If your stairs are already painted, you could mask off the "runner" area and paint it in a contrasting color—say white, with a blue or a Shaker-style brick red strip.

A bare wood "runner" is most practical for cleaning: either brush or vacuum off any dust, and follow with a damp cloth and detergent. Don't wax or polish the runner part since this will make it precariously slippery.

If the banisters and spindles of your staircase are in good condition, preserve it with a wax polish. If not, don't worry that you're being cruel to a good piece of mahogany; cover it up with a coat of eggshell paint.

ingredients

* ✱ Walls painted in white latex flat
* ✱ Woodwork painted in white eggshell paint
* ✱ Stairs sanded and painted with white floor paint, bar a central strip to look like a runner
* ✱ Floors sanded and painted with white floor paint
* ✱ Mahogany banister and spindles sanded and waxed
* ✱ A fab dress for making a glamorous descent

tip **TREAD CAREFULLY** If you want to paint your stairs all over and still fit in family life, there is a way! Starting at the top, paint every other stair. While the paint is drying, use the alternate unpainted stairs. When the paint is completely dry, the other steps can be painted.

big ideas

BEAN GREEN WALLS AND OVERSIZED FLOWER HEADS GIVE A RELAXED ORGANIC FLAVOR TO A NARROW HALLWAY, WHERE SPACE AND LIGHT ARE AT A PREMIUM.

Some old houses have narrow entrance halls. Although a hallway is theoretically useful in channelling traffic past the living room, a very narrow one presents a few decorating and practical problems. It can easily become cluttered and too cramped to serve as a convenient thoroughfare in a family home. Because embarking on structural rearrangements is out of the question for most of us, it is financially more agreeable to make the most of what you've got.

Start by maximizing the available light sources. A glazed front door and fanlight will make the most of any natural daylight, particularly crucial during short winter days.

Although white does open up a restricted space, consider an organic hue, like this bean green on the walls. It is pleasing to the eye and echoes the natural greenery of the front yard—a sort of uninterrupted color flow from exterior to interior. Shots of pink, provided by the blowsy hydrangeas, add contrast and accentuate the natural feel.

It makes perfect sense in a long, skinny hallway to install a narrow table that will house baskets underneath for footballs, rubber boots, and all the usual outdoor things.

There's nothing like going over the top with a giant globe paper lantern—a real sixties retro idea, which still looks good. Now, you may think this is the last thing anyone would want in a teeny-weeny hallway, but, like magic, large objects in small spaces can actually increase the perceived sense of space. Try the same trick by putting a huge mirror in a small living room or a king-size bed in a small spare room. By the way, this trickery of the eye does not work in reverse—a minuscule light in a big hall, will look, well, pretty pathetic.

For protection against a brigade of dirty feet, fit a heavy-duty doormat over wooden pine boards that have been sanded and sealed. The floor will deal with an enormous amount of wear and tear and need only the minimum of upkeep with a mop-down and occasional rewaxing.

tip

HOW TO PAINT

✻ Dip the brush in the paint to cover half the bristle length. Wipe off any excess paint on the side of the can.
✻ Lay the paint on by applying a horizontal band approximately 8 in. (20cm) wide, and brush out sideways. Finish with light strokes in a crisscross pattern.
✻ Hold a small paintbrush like a pencil, but hold a large paintbrush like a table tennis bat.
✻ If using a roller, load it with paint by pushing it back and forth in the front of the tray, then do the same on the slope of the tray to spread the paint evenly over the roller.
✻ Roll slowly and evenly until the area is covered.
✻ Do not load the roller with too much paint, and take the roller off the wall carefully to prevent splashing.

ingredients

✻ Front door with glazed panels and a fanlight to make the most of the limited light

✻ Walls painted in bean green latex flat

✻ Wooden floorboards, sanded and waxed

✻ Heavy-duty doormat fixed like carpeting

✻ Long, narrow wooden hall table

✻ Large glass vase with the last of the summer hydrangeas

✻ Oversized paper globe lantern

smart and simple

HARDWORKING GINGHAM AND CERAMIC TILES FOR A STYLISH ENTRANCE.

Treat your hall as you would any other room, and make it as pleasingly functional as you can. It is true that you don't linger in an entrance as long as in other spaces, but it creates the first impression of your home and needs to beguile guests.

Creating a sense of space and openness in the hallway is key. Here it has been achieved with fresh white paint, a bare tiled floor, and a large mirror, also painted white, to reflect the light back from the glazed doorway.

Another idea for a hard-wearing floor that doesn't necessarily need to be protected by rugs and runners, is linoleum tiles, which can be laid in a simple checker board pattern. You could also consider tough studded rubber tiles or even cork, which is making something of a comeback.

Seize upon any chance to play and punch in some great color with soft furnishings. I have dressed a couple of sixties wooden side chairs in pull-on purple gingham covers. The fabric is washable and so will easily cope with the moment when little Johnny drops his ice-cream cone. Besides covering side chairs, which can be pulled in as reserves around the dining table, you could also cover an uninteresting hall table in a piece of striped ticking or checked or plaid cloth, edged with velvet ribbon for a really smart look.

To reiterate: damage-proof elements are crucial in the hallway. Buggy wheels spell death to anything precious or antique, so I would not advise displaying your fanciest pieces. Instead, opt for church candles on a hallway table for Christmas; or in summer, stuff vases with sprigs of rosemary to set the scene for feasting out in the garden. Simple touches like fresh flowers can cheer up even the most impersonal hallway.

ingredients

* **Walls** painted in white latex flat
* **Woodwork** painted in white eggshell
* **Large mirror** painted in white eggshell to reflect the available light
* **Industrial-style enamel pendant lampshade**
* **Sixties beech chairs** dressed in gingham covers (see page 122)
* **Floor covered** with antique ceramic tiles

period feature

If you are restoring and renovating an old house and are lucky enough to have intact ceramic floor tiles, it's likely that they'll need a really good clean. Detergent and water alone will not be strong enough, so go to a building materials store to buy a specialist cleaner that will remove ingrained dirt. The floor can then be sealed with a clear, matte varnish, which will keep maintenance down to mopping as necessary. Cracked or loose tiles can be fixed using a two-part epoxy resin adhesive. Remove any dust and dirt from the tile spaces before commencing repairs.

cool country

STYLISH TEXTURES THAT ARE TOUGH AND HARD-WEARING.

Rural life is often fantasized about by urbanites, who rarely have to grapple with power cuts, uninvited insects, or little people watching TV while wearing rubber boots caked in mud (far too mucky for the lifestyle magazines). With this last point in mind, it is prudent to choose a robust floor covering for the thoroughfares in a country abode. The sealed terracotta floor tiles seen here are perfect for dealing with dirt.

Don't throw up your hands (chapped from all that fresh air and digging) at the thought of laying a lovely white floor runner to skim the length of a well-trafficked hallway or passage. There is a trick: buy the cotton variety. Rag rugs are equally good. When necessary, throw the rug in the washing machine, or soak it in the bath tub, and leave it to dry al fresco. Watch out for strong colors, though, as the dye may run.

The wash-and-wear approach also applies to the wall surfaces. I have known everything from sticky handprints to pig fat to leave their marks on the walls. It is always useful to have a can of latex paint on hand for dealing with such irritations.

Keep the entrance space free from excess boxes, laundry, piles of books and toys to suggest an orderly visual flow. A simple table—a beat-up secondhand buy, painted with a single coat of latex paint and then unevenly rubbed down with sandpaper for an aged effect—and some flowers are always appropriate. Placing a chair, table, or even a mirror at the end of the space creates a pleasing sense of perspective.

ingredients

* **Walls and woodwork painted in white latex flat**
* Terracotta tiled floor
* Side table painted in latex flat and rubbed down with sandpaper for a rustic feel
* Washable white cotton floor runner
* Metal lantern for candles
* Flowers in a simple glass pitcher

tip PAINTING WALLS Before painting, wash interior walls down using a sponge, and apply an undercoat. Finish with two coats of latex flat. Work in 2-ft. (60cm) bands with a roller, starting in the top right-hand corner if you are right-handed or the top left-hand corner if you are left-handed and ending in the opposite bottom corner above the baseboard. Use a brush to "cut in" the narrow strip around the door and window frames after the main section of wall has been painted.

chill out

10 WAYS TO MAKE A RELAXING LIVING SPACE

1. Your chill-out space need not be a whole room, especially if your nest is small. A sofa dressed with squashy cushions and squeezed into a snug corner of a kitchen or dining room can work just as well.

2. Chairs look cool dressed in simple pull-on slipcovers, with maybe a tie here or a button detail there. Use tough machine-washable woven cotton including unbleached muslin. Natural linen is also good but creases, so it's not for the fussy. Preshrink all fabrics before use.

3. Buy the biggest sofa you can afford; a good one should have a solid hardwood frame with a sprung base and back. Secondhand buys from the forties or earlier might need bodywork, but they're made of sturdy stuff and will be cheaper than a modern equivalent.

4. Feather-filled cushions are soft and yielding; although they need plumping daily to maintain their shape, they are the best option. Do not bother with cheap foam cushions as they are not worth it for either looks or comfort.

5. I prefer calm, soft pools of light from table lamps with pretty shades trimmed with ribbons. Paper parchment shades are good. Dark walls absorb more light than paler ones, so choose the wattage of your bulbs accordingly. Try to use low-energy lightbulbs, which last longer and are more energy efficient than ordinary ones.

6. Build a blazing fire with smokeless fuel or logs. Sweep the chimney if it has not been used for some time. If your heating system uses cast-iron radiators, and you want colored walls, paint the radiators to match, using special radiator paint.

7. Sunny south-facing sitting rooms that let in lots of light are tremendously uplifting on winter days. In summer, cover them with sheer draw draperies to reduce heat and lower your air-conditioning bills.

8. Blue and white is my number one chill-out colour combo – it looks classic yet modern and never dates. Key elements include soft white, duck-egg blue or eau-de-nil walls teamed with striped cotton ticking and checks.

9. Use natural textures and scents for a living, breathing space. Try roughly woven baskets, fibrous rugs and woolly throws. Burn tea lights in jars or light a good scented candle (such as tuberose by Diptyque) that actually smells of what it claims to.

10. Wall-to-wall carpets don't suit a light and airy look, so stick to mats or rugs for added texture and warmth underfoot. Painted white floorboards are easy to achieve. (See page 90.)

big sofas are best

COMFY SEATING TO SPRAWL ON AND BLUE AND WHITE DETAILS ARE KEY INGREDIENTS FOR A LIGHT AND AIRY LIVING ROOM.

Divide the living room into a series of zones to create a more inviting and layered look. I like to position a slim table behind the sofa; this provides a focal point for the eye and a handy space for lamps—useful for reading by—and flowers. If this space is by a window, even better, as the eye is drawn to another area of interest outside.

On a technical note, think about installing floor-mounted electrical outlets to power centrally positioned lamps. If you're starting from scratch, it's worth roughly planning the arrangement of your furniture so that you know where the wiring needs to be routed. See pages 16–17 for tips on drawing up a simple plan.

Then there is the seating itself. Measure up before buying that great ship of a bargain sofa. It would be too, too awful to find that it won't squeeze through the front door, let alone negotiate hairpin turns around a narrow staircase. Having said that, it is possible to take out windows and hire a man with a winch to haul a really big sofa up to where you need it. It may be worth the effort and expense for a really well made piece that you intend to live with for years. Accessorize your sofa with several squashy cushions—never arranged in stiff rows—and maybe a throw.

Installing a big sofa or two eliminates the need to clutter up the rest of the room. Stick to essential items only. If your floor is bare, the space in front of the sofa where there might be a low table, or a big square footstool piled with favorite books, is the place to have a rug; choose something pretty in stripes, or sisal, or a gorgeous wool, to give texture and color.

If there's space, you could have two sofas facing each other. So much the better if there is a fireside beside which you can curl up on a drizzly Sunday afternoon.

ingredients

* Walls painted in white latex flat
* Woodwork painted in white eggshell
* Floorboards sanded and painted in white floor paint
* Sofa covered in washable white cotton slipcovers
* Blue-and-white striped cotton cushions
* Blue-and-white striped lampshades
* Sixties wooden coffee tables
* Fifties wirework side chairs
* White roller shades
* Woven wicker log baskets

tip

HOW TO PREPARE FOR PAINTING
* Dress in your oldest painting clothes, and wear protective headgear.
* Place the paint can on newspaper or a plastic sheet.
* Open the paint can with a screwdriver or a large coin.
* Stir the paint with a thick stick.
* Mix the paint with a circular up-and-down motion.
* Latex paint that has not been used for a while may have water on top; pour it away.
* An oil-based paint will have a skin, which should be cut off; sieve the remaining paint through an old pair of pantyhose.
* Thin the paint if very thick; use water for latex and mineral spirits for oil-based paints.

cool and modern

CHILL OUT WITH SIMPLE RETRO IDEAS.

Streamlined, modern, and functional sixties-style furniture is back in vogue and suits the mood for simple living. It's likely that parents and grandparents will be harboring some really cool relics from the era and might even be persuaded to part with them—my mother-in-law's Saarinen white tulip table and chairs are good examples. The secondhand furniture trade knows the value of these things well; consequently you have to look harder for bargains.

Do you remember when walls were lined with orange burlap and the groovy thing to do was make lampbases out of Chianti bottles encased in raffia? I suspect there won't be a revival of the latter, but I am all for choosing something rough and textural, such as burlap, in stone colors. I have also been toying with the idea of using cork wallpaper: a thin layer of amalgamated cork bonded to

ingredients

* **Walls papered with sixties-style geometric-print wallpaper**
* **Floor covered with seagrass matting**
* **Sixties-style sideboard**
* **Sixties-style pendant lampshade**
* **Vintage floor lamp**
* **Red canvas draperies**

backing paper, which has an organic look and will add color and texture to a room but maintain a contemporary look. I can see it looking really good in an eco house tucked away in the woods.

Watch for new interpretations of the sixties look, too. There are some great wallpapers around—a big, bold geometric pattern is a relatively cheap and easy way to make a stunning visual statement in a room.

Finally, the new wave of wallpapers includes photographic papers in which digital images are blown up and used across a whole wall. It's pretty expensive but does allow you to indulge in using your photographs and designs as inspiration.

Lighting is another area that is harking back to the swinging days of the sixties. There are some fabulous pendant lamps and hanging shades in molded plastic that will add that psychedelic edge to your living space.

tip

WALLPAPER PREP

YOU WILL NEED:
* Fold-up pasting table, which can be bought cheaply from a home center
* Pasting brush
* 10-in. (25cm) wide wallpaper hanging brush
* Bucket for paste
* Cloth and sponge for smoothing down and removing excess paste
* Seam roller for smoothing edges
* Long spirit level
* Wallpaper scissors
* Tape measure to work out the lengths of paper

childproof and stylish

WASHABLE STRIPES THAT CAN COPE WITH STICKY FINGERS.

It's not so scary, I promise you, to invest in pretty fabrics and attractive furnishing ideas in rooms that house the dangerous combination of a TV and children. My offspring like nothing more than curling up in front of "The Simpsons" with plates of something sweet and sticky—the remnants of which are usually smeared and crumbled over the chairs. I stoically whip off the covers and give them a good wash. Then when they're still a bit damp, I stretch them back over the seating to look good as new until the next sticky assault.

The key to a child-friendly interior is to make sure that all the furnishings in the room, even the rugs, are washable and that all surfaces can simply be wiped down. Use spongeable paint finishes for both walls and woodwork.

It might sound churlish in our child-centered times, but bedrooms apart, there is no need to infantilize your house with untidy piles of toys and playthings. Modern plastic toys are such an eyesore that they need suitable storage to allow you to put back some visual order at the end of the day. I recommend rigid white plastic boxes that can be stacked away in the corner, or old junk shop cupboards that can be painted and used for toys, games, videos, and DVDs.

Another option is to limit the amount of stuff your children have. Does your little darling really need ten My Scene dolls, plus their plastic surfer boyfriends, sports car, and film-star sized wardrobes?

ingredients

* **Walls painted in white latex flat**
* **Sanded and scrubbed wooden floorboards, painted with a dark stain**
* **Secondhand cupboards painted in white eggshell for storing videos and DVDs**
* **Armchairs covered in blue-and-white striped cotton slipcovers**
* **Washable cotton rugs**

tip

HOW TO PAINT A DOOR
* Wash door thoroughly and wedge open. Use a primer/undercoat and apply two top coats. Rub down the paintwork between each coat. Start in the top left-hand corner and paint in bands about 20 in. (50cm) wide. Work fast, so that the painted bits are joined while the paint is still wet.

ORDER TO PAINT A WINDOW
* 1 top sash
* 2 bottom sash
* 3 frame and rabbets
* 4 interior moldings of window
* 5 top and bottom
* 6 left and right
* 7 window frame
(For a neat finish, apply masking tape to edge of panes before painting, and scrape any stray paint off with a razor blade.)

unfussy florals

GIVE COUNTRY BUDS AND BLOOMS A CONTEMPORARY TWIST.

The clever way to do florals—a.k.a the traditional country house look—is not to do them to death. Blooms rioting and rambling across walls and every piece of furniture might be the preferred look of the queens of chintz, but to make it look modern you have to be restrained in execution. Here, only one wall has been papered with a blowsy rose-patterned paper, which makes it a cheaper option.

Combined with simple decorating details—a gingham-trimmed lampshade, a small secondhand sofa updated

with a pull-on cotton slipcover, green plaid cotton cushion covers, and spring bulbs in basic flowerpots—the effect is fresh and contemporary.

Going back to the lampshade; yes, this rather dated interior feature is having a renaissance. Usually associated with grandma's comfortable living room, the lampshade is returning in a rather more glamorous guise this time around.

The trick is not to rush to the attic to dig out your old peach ruched silk shade, pale, dull and so "yesterday." Choose color, pattern, trimmings, or a big, bold silhouette. Shades come in linen, silk, suede, velvet, and parchment—my favorite because it diffuses the light beautifully. Treat a lampshade like a gorgeous hat, and decorate it with ribbon, braids, and bows.

I love the vogue for floor lamps with fabulous shades; they look good in a dull corner and also give pleasing height. After years of concealed designer lighting, it's definitely time to put bold decorative lamps back on the agenda.

tip

HOW TO HANG WALLPAPER
* Start papering at one side of the largest window in the room, and work toward the door.
* If using a large-patterned paper, hang the first length over the fireplace or the focal point of the room, and work away from it in both directions so that the design is central and symmetrical.
* It is vital that the first piece of paper you hang be straight, as it will be the guide for all the rest. Use a spirit level to make a vertical, and mark it with pencil or chalk.
* Place the strip of wallpaper on the pasting table, apply the paste, and leave to soak.
* Fold the wallpaper into pleats.
* Position the paper along the edge of the vertical line.
* Butt the edges, and use a wallpaper brush to smooth into position, working from the center to the edges of paper to remove any bubbles.
* Crease the overlaps at the top and bottom of the wall, cut neatly with scissors, and brush back into place.
* Avoid squeezing paste out of joints.
* Wipe off excess paste while it is moist, using a clean, damp sponge.

ingredients
* Walls papered in rose-print wallpaper
* Floor covered with sisal matting and a wool rug
* Sixties wooden side table
* Wooden two-seater sofa covered in a white unbleached muslin cover
* Secondhand-store lampstand painted in white eggshell with a fabric shade trimmed with gingham (see page 151)

soft light by the fireside

THE ONLY WAY TO SURVIVE DEEP MID-WINTER IS BY TURNING YOUR NEST INTO A COZY RETREAT, WITH SIMPLE INDULGENCES LIKE TEA AND TOAST IN FRONT OF A LOG FIRE.

Deep, rich terracottas and muddy greens are traditional snug, curling-up-in-a-ball colors that work well in the shadows, but walls painted white are modern and light enhancing for wintry rooms.

The bigger the fireplace, the larger the blaze, which is why the small grates found in some old houses are worth enlarging to make simple, modern rectangular openings. A built-in mantelshelf is wide enough but not too wide for candles, art, mirrors, and, for those who like to appear busy, important invitations.

The choice of log baskets is crucial—the bigger and more roughly woven, the better. I put them beside the fireplace for a rural feel. Never buy those finished with wood stain— they might be really cheap, but they look shiny and unnatural. The safety police will note that firesides like this should never be left unattended.

If you're intending to install a new heating system, you might consider infloor heating (also called underfloor or radiant heating). This is especially desirable under tiled floors, which tend to be chilly underfoot. Infloor heating has long been used for new houses in Europe and is becoming increasingly popular in the United States. It is even, quiet, and invisible.

Pools of soft lamplight and candlelight are the best ways to make a winter room both look and feel snug. Slender lamp bases with simple paper shades are classic and survive any changes in lighting trends. Where possible, use 40 watt bulbs which are easier on the eyes then higher-wattage ones. The eco-conscious will know that low-energy bulbs last between five and ten times longer and use 75 percent less electricity than ordinary incandescent ones.

Just as my lightweight linen separates are returned to the back of the closet at the end of summer, my white sofa slipcovers are packed away to make way for soft pink heavy cotton ones that suit the wintry mood. For the scatter cushions, cotton in pink plaid and a floral sprig print give a modern take on the country look.

ingredients

* Walls in white latex flat
* Terracotta tiled floor
* Large, open fireplace
* Logs in woven baskets
* Blue and white striped cotton rug
* Pink plaid and floral print cotton cushions
* Slender lamp base and simple paper lampshade
* Tea and toast

tile file

Terracotta tiles are fantastically hard-wearing and, when bought from a local source, are much cheaper than if they are transported from afar. Terracotta is super-absorbent, so any spills will be permanently visible unless you seal the tiles as soon as they're laid. I have found that applying two coats of linseed oil provides protection against red wine, grease, and the usual domestic stains. Before applying the oil, clean the unsealed tiles with a damp cloth to remove any surface dust. Using a brush, apply the oil to the tiles in a thin layer. Allow to dry for approximately 12 hours, then apply a second coat—two coats should suffice. Thereafter, maintenance is minimal—a daily sweep and a weekly mop down with a mild detergent.

make the difference

color

Nothing is harder than getting color right in the home. Most of us have little color sense, so the best thing is to go to your local home center and grab those paint cards with edited ranges, rather than the big ones with a daunting choice of hundreds of colors. You can now buy sample jars of some paints. Try your chosen color on a small area of wall, then watch to see how it changes during natural daylight and then at night in artificial light.

Color alters depending on the light that falls on it. Daylight tends to be bluer than artificial light, which is more constant, as it isn't moving like the sun.

❝Change your look with just a lick of paint. ❞

North-facing rooms are darker and need warm colors like soft yellows; south-facing rooms can have harsh shadows and glare, so cooler blues and greens will work well (wraparound white can be overpowering, so it is best to use with splashes of contrasting color).

Rooms facing east are warmer in the morning with more yellow light from the sunrise, which cools as the day progresses; west-facing rooms are best at sunset and feel colder in the morning; walls that have direct light appear lighter, and walls that surround a window fall into shadow, so colors will appear darker.

eat

10 WAYS TO MAKE A PRACTICAL KITCHEN

1 Open shelves provide invaluable storage above kitchen worktops, giving easy access to pots, pans, and tableware. Use lengths of pine and simple brackets, which can be given a lick of paint or simply sealed.

2 My children are messy cooks, and so am I, which is why the floor needs to be as robust and stain resistant as possible. Waxed floorboards, sealed terracotta tiles, and good old-fashioned linoleum are all surfaces that can withstand a battering.

3 If you inherit a fitted kitchen you hate, don't rip it out. Revamp it. Simply replace the doors; basic tongue-and-groove makes a far cheaper option than starting all over again.

4 Less is more. Resist the temptation to accumulate kitchen clutter. Most cooking tasks can be executed with the minimum— Le Creuset pans, several wooden spoons, a large stainless steel pasta pot, sharp knives, and a basic food processor.

5 Work surfaces that work. Beech and maple are excellent. Beware wet pans, which leave black rings. Marble is fabulous, as it doesn't encourage bug growth, but it hates lemon juice and other acids, which produce opaque stains. Stainless steel is lovely, but perfectionists may fret over scratches that are all part of ordinary wear and tear.

6 Good task lighting. Resist the urge to pepper the ceiling with downlighters. Restrict spots and pendant lights to the area directly above the work surface. Strip lighting under an eye-level shelf is also worth considering for chopping and mixing tasks.

7 A decent-sized table. Buy the biggest your space allows. Some swear by round ones—good for bay windows—but I prefer rectangular shapes. My sturdy table is used by all the family for homework and writing, and has often squeezed in twelve for loud Sunday lunches.

8 Windows—to let natural light and air in, as well as kitchen fug out— are key for the room at the heart of the home. I chose to put my kitchen in what was a living room, rather than settle for the original, but dark and gloomy, kitchen space.

9 Everyone should have an old-fashioned pantry, keeping cheese at the correct room temperature and yesterday's apple crisp cool. If you've got one, count yourself fortunate.

10 Simple table accessories. White cotton or linen tablecloths and napkins, cream candles, and a vase with a rose or two from the garden are all you need for a simple feast. Plus, of course, some wholesome, fresh foodie ingredients.

budget modern

HOW TO MAKE A KITCHEN PRACTICAL, SIMPLE, AND STYLISH USING READYMADE CABINETS.

Status-symbol kitchens can cost a fortune. The antidote to this conspicuous consumption in culinary matters is to assemble your own kitchen cabinets, using prefabricated units. These are manufactured in a huge range of materials, from particleboard and MDF (medium-density fiberboard), at the cheaper end of the range, to plywood (often with solid-wood doors) to solid hardwoods such as cherry, ash, and oak. There's also a great variety of storage units available, including slide-out pantry shelves and cabinets that fit into corners. If you can only afford MDF or particleboard interiors, you can visually upgrade these with handsome stained wood facings and some classy hardware.

Plan the kitchen carefully, using graph or quadrille paper to make a scale drawing. When measuring, allow for any pipe work that might need to be incorporated in the cabinet space, such as under-sink plumbing.

When space is tight, a single run of basic units comprising sink, countertop, and range is most useful, especially in rooms of narrow proportions. Together with a large catering-

ingredients

* Prefabricated kitchen units, including cabinets and drawers
* Basic stainless-steel sink and faucet
* Hanging rail made from a metal pole cut to size
* Reclaimed wood shelving painted in white eggshell
* Backsplash made from basic white rectangular ceramic tiles
* Walls painted in white latex semigloss
* Wooden blockboard work surface
* Industrial-style glass pendant lights

tip

FLATPACK PANIC

* Allow plenty of time; don't even think about rushing it.
* Allow plenty of space, and make sure the finished item will fit into the room it's destined for.
* Make sure you have all the correct tools before you start.
* Unpack everything carefully, and check off all the parts, looking for any damage.
* Lay out and identify all the pieces before assembling.
* Don't force any joints or screws if they aren't fitting.
* Wait until the end to tighten all the screws in case of problems that would entail undoing all your work.

style oven and a refrigerator and freezer, this simple arrangement will cover most families' basic kitchen needs.

Seeking out practical, yet good-looking materials from widely available sources does not mean skimping on quality. Building supplies stores offer basic but honest stainless-steel sinks and white ceramic tiles.

A chunky shelf made from reclaimed pine, painted in tough white eggshell and fitted with new brackets at eye level provides easy access to key cooking utensils and plain china. Beneath this is a metal pole—bought from a building supplies stores, cut with a hacksaw, and attached with hanging rail fixings—with butchers' hooks for hanging scissors, colanders, graters, and other essential equipment—an idea borrowed from restaurant kitchens.

The wall above is painted in white latex semigloss, a waterproof surface from which it is easier to remove cooking stains than an ordinary latex flat.

The wooden blockboard countertop is practical and tactile; it can be bought by the yard and fitted using screws. Rather than being solid, blockboard is made up of many small pieces of wood molded together. To keep countertops in good order, sand before use and seal with several coats of wood sealer. If any black mould marks appear, simply repeat the process every few months.

retro style

COOL GREENS AND BLUES, SECONDHAND KITCHEN CHAIRS, AND DOTTED FABRICS CREATE A FRESH TAKE ON THE VINTAGE LOOK.

My grandmother's kitchen houses a large dresser loaded with stacks of plates and cup hooks hung with tattered recipes, tea towels, and dog leads. How homely and reassuring. It is no wonder that the retro look is so appealing to the frazzled twenty-first-century homemaker.

The kitchen in my own home was once the domain of Betty: she prepared the daily tea at 4p.m. on the dot, with trays spread with starched white linen and wholesome cakes. This is a peaceful, productive room, so I chose a soft green color in eggshell which echoes the past, yet at the same time looks contemporary. Color is key to creating a nostalgic mood (think soft greens, creams, and gray). The texture of the color is important, too, with matter

chalky surfaces looking more old-fashioned. The color is used as a device to unify the walls and the furniture—the dresser and cabinets are painted in eggshell, whereas the walls are in latex flat.

To get the dresser look, you can make do with a robust freestanding 3-ft. (1m)-high wooden cupboard with drawers (look in salvage yards for old school and office furniture and the bases of dressers that have been separated from their shelves). Put up rows of shelves above, and paint all the pieces in the same color for a unified effect.

Furniture and accessories all help to create the retro feel. Painted secondhand chairs are exactly right for a vintage flavor. Sanding and painting woodwork is a bargain way to update any down-at-heel chairs. Do check, though, for tiny woodworm holes in the wood. Do not buy any item if it is riddled, or treat with a woodworm preparation if there are only a few. Look for striped, checked, dotted, and pretty floral fabrics to make into chair covers, simple curtains, and cloths. Use plain white china and tableware, or seek out authentic retro green and cream enameled tinware. (I find the stacking tins very useful.) This kind of kitchenware often appears in secondhand shops and on market stalls.

paint problems?

PARTICLES IN THE PAINT: Caused by dust or inadequate wiping down after sanding. To remedy, rub the paint down with a fine-grit abrasive paper once dry, and apply a fresh coat.

DRIPS AND RUNS: Caused by overloading the paintbrush and not spreading the paint out far enough. To remedy, follow the instructions given above.

BLISTERS: Caused by water vapor from damp present before painting, or that crept into the wood after. Not noticeable in cold weather, but in heat the water evaporates and blisters appear. When only a few blisters, remove and fill, rub down, and repaint surface. If there are too many, start again.

WRINKLES: A crinkled effect that occurs when gloss paint is applied too thickly or to a badly prepared surface. Strip off, sand, and repaint.

FLAKING: If flakes occur in new paint, the surface was badly prepared. If flakes occur in old paint, it can be caused by rot due to damp, frost, or hot sun. Strip off, prepare, and repaint.

ingredients

* Walls painted in soft green latex flat
* Simple wooden dresser painted in soft green eggshell
* Wooden floorboards sanded and painted in white floor paint
* Junk kitchen chairs sanded and painted in powder blue eggshell
* Tablecloth in dot-print cotton (see page 144)
* Dot-print apron (see page 130)
* 1940s green and cream enameled tinware picked up from market stalls

cook's kitchen

STAINLESS STEEL IS AS MUCH AT HOME IN THE DOMESTIC KITCHEN AS IT IS IN THE CATERING ENVIRONMENT.

Stainless steel is so strong and practical that commercial kitchens, which must be rigorously maintained, choose it for everything from sinks to cooking pots. On the domestic front, it makes good sense to consider the use of stainless steel for sinks, shelving, and countertops.

The highest grade stainless steel is expensive. For a budget option, flick through your local business directory to find suppliers of catering kit from commercial kitchens that have gone bust or are upgrading. Don't be put off by the fact that these establishments are usually sited in grimy yards under railroad arches, they can be very good sources of sinks and countertops, shelves, or stainless-steel-fronted catering fridges, which can all be put to domestic use.

For something functional that doesn't cost a fortune, commission a catering supplier to make a kitchen for you. It will be more basic than the average kitchen, but it will be stylishly utilitarian. Here, in the home of a professional pastry chef, one wall of a smallish kitchen has been kitted out with a made-to-order sink, countertop, and shelving arrangement in stainless steel.

A key feature of these cabinets is the shallow drawers that allow for the storage of cups and cutlery. As in commercial kitchens, the sink is wide and deep for washing big pans and stacks of plates. It is possible to increase countertop space in an arrangement like with a custom-made chopping board that rests over the edges of the sink.

Simple triangular brackets support two rows of shelves, which hold saucepans, casseroles, and a food mixer—the mighty gadget with which Jonny prepares his lemon cakes, iced coffee cakes, gloriously crisp pear tarts, and other mouth-watering desserts. Jonny is a lofty individual who has no problem grabbing his gear from the upper shelves. For most of us, however, keeping shelves low, so that the most-used tools are within arm's reach is more ergonomic.

Recessed halogen downlighters are fitted above the work surface, and there is linoleum flooring, which is maintained with a damp mop and detergent. In order for cooking operations to be carried out efficiently, a gas oven and wooden preparation table are sited opposite the sink area.

Despite its name, stainless steel can be stained by various substances—salt, acidic food, bleach, and some detergents. Wipe down regularly with lemon juice or a cut lemon to brighten the surface. Don't fuss too much about stains; they are part of the normal wear and tear.

ingredients

* **Walls painted in pale pink latex semigloss paint**
* **Stainless-steel kitchen cabinets and shelving**
* **Floor covered in creamy yellow linoleum**
* **Halogen downlighters over work surface**
* **Fold-up wooden drainer**
* **Heavy-based pots and pans to create culinary magic**

tip HOW TO LIVE WITH LINO If laying sheet linoleum onto a wood floor, you must either pull out or punch in any proud nails. An underlay should be laid and stuck in position with lino adhesive. Lino can be bonded to concrete or stone in the same way, provided the floor is clean, dry, and level. It is important to seal lino; washing an unsealed lino with hot water and detergent tends to open the pores and remove the oils blended into the lino during manufacture, so that it becomes increasingly difficult to clean. Seal with a specialist cleaner for best protection, but wash with detergent before sealing, in order to remove the manufacturer's protective film.

country without the chintz

PLAIN TONGUE-AND-GROVE DETAIL, SIMPLE ACCESSORIES, AND A BIG WOODEN TABLE ARE THE ESSENTIAL INGREDIENTS FOR THE MODERN COUNTRY KITCHEN.

There are some rustic romantics who can't get enough of country life: laundry slowly drying on the overhead airer, hot bread straight from the oven, and steamy dog baskets. If the traditional farmhouse feel is not your cup of tea, however, a more modern, pared-down country look is workable—whether you're living in the sticks or wedged between a pizza parlor and a pool hall.

There is a simple L-shaped run of kitchen cabinets—the tongue-and-groove detail is country without being cutesy—with cabinets for storing pots pans, cleaning materials, and food, and the obviously practical close arrangement of oven, sink, and dishwasher. Also in tongue-and-groove, a basic slimline cabinet with double doors and shelving is wide enough to take the biggest dinner plates (any wider and it would take up too much space and look clumsy). To make the most of the natural light seeping in from the window, the sink is positioned below the window, for dishwashing with a view.

A work surface in unpolished creamy marble fits in comfortably with the natural, understated look. Similarly, the tiled terracotta floor—sealed with several coats of linseed oil to repel red wine, olive oil, and other cooking culprits—has all the components of country style: it's rough in texture, earthy in color, and hard-wearing. (Heavy tiles like this are not advisable when the weight-bearing ability of flooring above ground level is an issue.)

The key accessories that bring this simple look together are a solid chestnut table and folding chairs that can also be moved outside (the table has a detachable top) when the sun shines, functional glass preserving jars for storing dry foods, and a large metal florists' bucket filled with heady scented tuberoses.

ingredients

* Wooden tongue-and-groove doors and cabinets painted in white eggshell
* Walls painted in white latex flat
* Terracotta-tiled floor
* Marble work surface
* Open shelving
* Simple glass preserving jars for storage
* Simple chestnut dining table large enough to seat ten people
* Fold-up wood and metal slatted chairs in white
* Stems of white tuberoses for a summery feel (their heady scent thickens as dusk falls)

tip

HOW TO PUT UP A BASIC SHELF
* Mark the position of the shelf at several points along its length, using a spirit level to make sure it is straight and level.
* Drill two $1/4$-in. (6mm) holes in the wall with a masonry drill using two shelf brackets as a guide for positioning.
* Insert $1/4$-in. (6mm) anchors into the drilled holes. The anchors should be flush with the wall surface.
* Using four $1^1/2$-in. (40mm) screws, fix the brackets to the wall.
* Attach the shelf to the brackets using four $1^1/4$-in. (32mm) finishing nails.

crisp blue and white

EAT WELL IN A SIMPLE, UNCLUTTERED, BLUE-AND-WHITE DINING SPACE.

To make sure the important business of eating and drinking is the main focus of a meal, the ingredients for my perfect dining room are simple: White walls, white woodwork, and simple roller shades in blue-and-white striped cotton create a blank canvas that serves as the backdrop for the food.

A sanded and waxed wooden floor not only is practical—easily cleaned after a long Sunday dinner or the most boisterous children's party—but creates a feeling of spaciousness even in small areas.

Simple Shaker-style beech chairs, popular in the sixties, are becoming increasingly sought after—so much so that there is now a roaring trade in them on eBay. I have managed to buy them for a song, however, from ordinary secondhand stores whose owners were unaware of their collectability.

Blue-and-white cotton checks look fresh, so use a length of this fabric to make a simple tablecloth. Or, if you feel your chairs aren't up to scratch, sew your own simple pull-on slipcovers.

Set the table with plain white china and simple glassware—elements that will not detract from the delicacies being served up to eat.

When it's cold and wintry outside, pots of narcissi and amaryllis bought inexpensively from local florists bring spring color and scent, while the shadow-intensifying candlelight softens the mood and inspires conversation.

ingredients

* Walls painted in white latex flat
* Wooden floorboards sanded and waxed
* Blue-and-white striped cotton roller shades
* Prefabricated pine table painted in undercoat and two coats of white eggshell
* 1960s beech dining chairs
* Blue-and-white checked tablecloth
* Candles on the table
* Amaryllis and narcissi in flowerpots

tip

HOW TO SAND A FLOOR
* Set aside an entire weekend for sanding a floor; don't think you can do it all in a day.
* Move everything out of the room to clear the floor.
* Rent a sander with a drum and an edge sander.
* Level the floor by removing all protruding tacks, and hammer any floor nails below the surface.
* Wear goggles and a face mask.
* Always allow the sander to move forward; don't let it stand still.
* Start sanding with a medium-grade paper, and finish with fine.
* When sanding, move along the length of the floorboards, never across them.
* Move the edge sander parallel with and close to the baseboards and along the floorboards.
* Vacuum and mop the freshly sanded floor to remove any dust before painting, varnishing, or sealing.

sleep

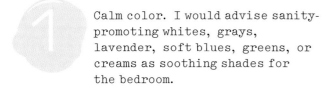

10 WAYS TO MAKE A CALMING BEDROOM

1. Calm color. I would advise sanity-promoting whites, grays, lavender, soft blues, greens, or creams as soothing shades for the bedroom.

2. Soft textures. Goosedown comforters and pillows ensure a good night's sleep. For additional warmth, padding and body cosseting, why not use a traditional feather bed (which fits between the mattress and bottom sheet)?

3. Life is too short to iron bed sheets. Fold while still partly damp, and place on top of the drier while its working and warm; fold and refold until dry. Or leave to flap dry on a clothesline and put straight onto the bed.

4. Comfort underfoot. Early-morning feet don't appreciate icy cold surprises. Even if you desire bare ceramic or wooden floors, be kind to your toes with a cotton bedside rug or natural fiber mat.

5. Invest in a good firm mattress. For back support, try a hand-tufted mattress stuffed with cotton and wool felt. Turn it every few months to prevent it from sagging where you sleep. Lay a blanket between the sheet and mattress to protect it and to give a smooth underside for the bottom sheet. It is also extra toasty in winter.

6. Good things to help you sleep: Lavender pillows stored in the linen closet impart their herby scent. Traditional hot water bottles in wooly covers warm sheets in winter.

7. Think big bed. Even if your room's dimensions are limited, a bigger bed gives you a greater surface area to work, rest, and play on. If you're bothered about storage, invest in a bed frame with space beneath for boxes and crates to stow away bedroom clutter.

8. Every bed needs a side table with books, a clock, and a small vase of tulips, roses, or, perhaps, garden herbs. Bedside lamps trimmed with ribbons and bows are making a comeback; the prettier and girlier, the better. See page 150 for a pretty lampshade idea.

9. Good storage. Keep the bedroom clutter free. Reorganize your closets, possibly adding a shelf or two. You may need to have some extra closets built in the room. Or buy an armoire, for an attractive solution to the storage problem.

10. Poor sleepers benefit from blackout shades or lined draperies to keep out early morning light. Plain roller or Roman shades can be pulled down permanently to diffuse the light and afford privacy. White cotton, blue-and-white ticking, or floaty muslin drops with ribbon or tab ties are simple to run up on the sewing machine.

attic retreat

USE WHITE TO CREATE LIGHT AND AIRY WRAPAROUND COLOR.

Attic rooms are a godsend in households where the domestic habits and musical preferences of the teenage members clash with those of their parents.

When considering an attic space as a bedroom option, you must obviously make sure that the roof is well insulated and lined. This can be achieved by covering the space between the battens with strips of roofing felt or plastic sheeting, then nailing a suitable wallboard to the battens to form the ceiling. Adequate light is also an issue. It could involve the addition of skylights or a new dormer window construction; this may need a permit, so check your local building codes.

In this snug teen loft space, roof and walls are clad in tongue-and-groove paneling—boat-shed style—in keeping with the oarsman activities of the sixteen-year-old resident. As part of a general overhaul of the roof, extra light has been punched in, here, with a new double-glazed Velux window, an off-the-shelf purchase that is relatively cheap to buy and have installed.

Painting the entire space white, using eggshell on the walls and ceiling and specialist floor paint on the floorboards, not only is a stylistic consideration, but also is effective at making the space appear much lighter, in view of its low levels of natural light.

Then there is the issue of the loadbearing capability of an attic floor. To prevent a fast descent through to the rooms below, it will be necessary, for example, to lay new floor timbers on the joists if the existing floor is made of only thin plywood. This is an area which a good building contractor should be competent to advise on.

ingredients

* Walls clad in pine tongue-and-groove paneling painted in white eggshell
* Wooden floorboards sanded and painted in white floor paint
* Swedish-style wooden bed
* Blue-and-white striped bed linens
* Bedroom chair with pull-on washable unbleached muslin cover with button detail
* Washable white cotton rag rug

tip

HOW TO PREPARE WOODWORK

* Wash all woodwork down with water and a little detergent.
* If stripping damaged or flaking paint, use a blowtorch (cheap but a fire risk), a hot-air gun (heavy but safer and better for large areas), or a chemical stripper (expensive and noxious but good for small areas and moldings—there are solvent, caustic, and peel-off varieties).
* Fill all holes and cracks with wood filler.
* Sand and then treat with a wood primer after rubbing down.

spare and calm

FREE YOUR SLEEP SPACE AND YOUR HEAD WITH CLEVER STORAGE SOLUTIONS.

One of my many unruly habits, along with slicing bread unevenly, is not putting my clothes away—so that by the end of the week there is an enormous heap draped over the bedroom chair. Tidying all this up slices into my cherished Saturday lie-in time, tucked up with toast and strong coffee. But at least I am very lucky to have decent closet space in which to decant the chaos.

When my bedroom is uncluttered, it is such a freeing place to be, and one in which I can think more clearly when trying to keep early morning worries from spiraling out of proportion.

Having exhausted the space in my small closet, I had to buy or build more storage in the room itself. Fortunately, the bedroom has two alcoves on either side of a fireplace, and so the solution of building two extra closets here was an obvious one. So as not to intrude into the room, they are quite shallow (just 18 in. [45cm] deep), with hanging rails fixed at right angles to the back walls, so that clothes can be hung comfortably. We used 1-in. (2.5cm)- thick particleboard for the frame and doors, and $^3/_8$-in. (1cm) for a simple molding on the doors. Once they were painted with an undercoat and three coats of eggshell, no one could guess that this is particleboard rather than wood. Above the closets there is shelf space, which, when I get around to it, I will fill with my favorite Spanish baskets to make extra storage.

Other useful ideas include those fabric hangers with pockets that are good for stashing away lingerie and small accessories. Low wooden benches make the most of space below—so that you can have several vertical rows for shoes. To keep moths from breakfasting on your favorite knitwear, I suggest investing in stout plastic clothes covers and hanging pieces of fragrant cedar wood—an eco moth deterrent—inside.

ingredients

* **Built-in closets sanded and painted in white eggshell**

* **Wooden floorboards sanded and painted in white floor paint**

* **Curtain rod painted white**

* **Tie curtain in blue-and-white ticking (see page 146)**

* **White cotton roller shade**

* **White chair covers**

* **Patchwork cushion**

tip

HOW TO PAINT WOODWORK

* Prime any new or stripped wood. Use stain- blocking sealer to paint the knots in softwood like pine before priming. Use an aluminum primer for exterior softwood, wood stripped by the blowtorch, hardwood, stained wood, and wood with preservative.
* Fill all cracks and holes with wood filler, and rub down before priming.
* Combined primers and undercoats are available, which mean you can dispense with the undercoat stage and go straight on to covering the wood with one or two layers of top coat.

modern florals

KEY GUEST ROOM DETAILS ARE SPLASHES OF COLOR AND NURTURING TEXTURES.

Papering walls is no longer a major felony, so what's to stop you from decorating one wall with a fabulous floral wallpaper? It will add color and detail without going over the top. Big patterns often work really well in small spaces, such as a guest bedroom, where pink roses gallop across the walls without looking in the least bit grannyish.

The secret is to mix in other fresh and contemporary elements, such as a basic Hollywood bed—this is not the place for elaborately padded and grand headboards—dressed in a hip pink trimmed sheet and cozy dyed purple cotton blanket. More splashes of modern color could include a roller shade trimmed with lime green velvet ribbon, a lamp decorated with pink ball fringe and a dressing table wearing a floaty pink and white skirt.

Along with pleasing colors, the comfort factor is a key element when it comes to making your guests feel nurtured and spoiled. Crisp cotton sheets and layers of wooly blankets will deal with their immediate needs. There should also be adequate space for hanging up clothes (make sure the closet has enough free hangers), a bedside table, and a small armchair dressed in a pretty slipcover, and maybe a table for working at or applying makeup.

Flowers are always cheering when you stumble in from a punishing journey—not a huge vaseful, but perhaps a glass with three or four tulips or just one gorgeous rose. These, plus the warm glow from a bedside lamp, a pitcher of water, a few books, and fresh, fluffy towels will do perfectly.

If the room hasn't been used for a while, remember to open the windows and give it a good airing for a few hours.

ingredients

* **Walls** papered in floral wallpaper
* **Table** sanded and painted, with voile skirt (see page 126)
* **Roman shades** edged with green ribbon
* **White cotton bed sheets** dyed pink (see page 148)
* **Dyed cotton blanket** (see also page 148)
* **Bedside lamp** trimmed with pink ball fringe (see page 150)

tip

TIPS FOR WALLPAPERING
* Check that every roll of paper has the same batch number and that there are no variations in color or faults.
* Walls to be papered should be clean, firm, and dry.
* Rub down any paint on walls with sandpaper.
* Scrape powdery or flaky areas, and paint with size, leaving them to dry completely.
* Leave new plaster to dry out for six months before papering.
* If walls are uneven, apply lining paper (from specialist retailers) and leave up to 12 hours to dry before papering.
* Some paper needs to be left with the paste on it for a period of time before hanging to allow the paste to soak into the paper and to prevent air bubbles.

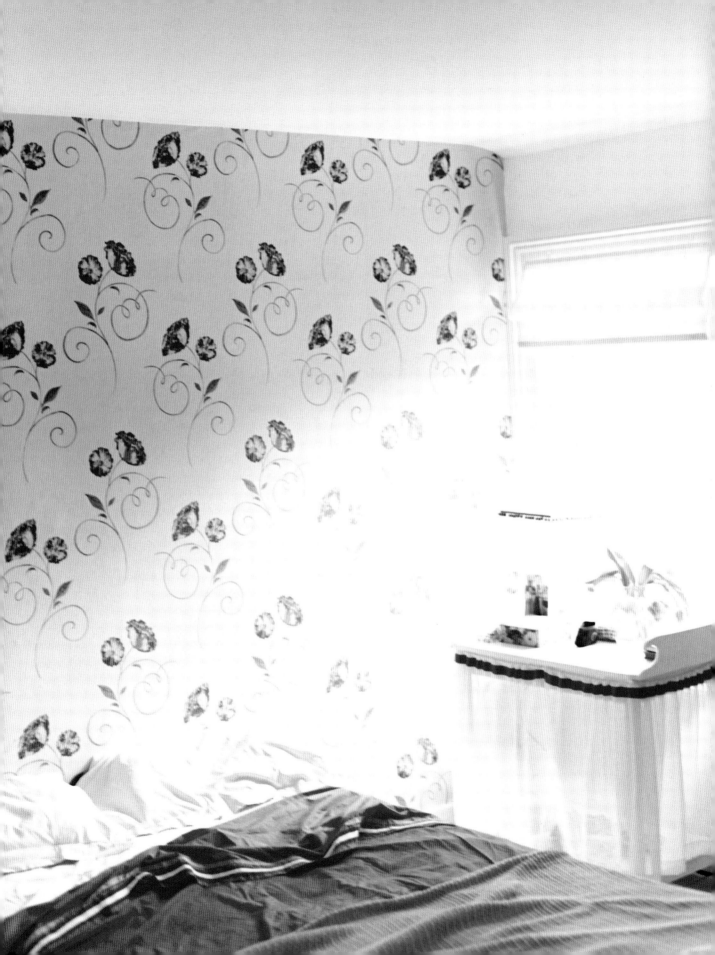

bed heaven

NATURAL TEXTURES AND GARDEN GREENS ARE SOOTHING BEDROOM ELEMENTS.

Soft bean green is a soothing, non-confrontational color idea to decorate with in the bedroom. In this pretty bedroom, filled with early morning summer light, lighter and darker tones of the same color sourced from a standard paint chart have been washed over the walls in latex flat and in a tough durable eggshell finish to update a Shaker-style prefabricated wooden four-poster.

This natural, from-the-vegetable-garden green makes white bed linens look crisp and punchy and is also an undemanding backdrop for accentuating colorful accessories and bedside flowers. Using other natural textures, such as rough seagrass matting, and a bedside bunch of flowers stuffed in a basic drinking glass helps to complete a harmonious and understated sleep sanctuary.

ingredients

* Walls painted in sage green latex flat

* Terracotta tiled floor

* Floor covered with a seagrass mat

* Wooden four-poster bed sanded and painted

* Painted secondhand chair sanded and painted

* Flexible thirties-style metal lamp

* Lavender water cologne to freshen the sheets

more handy paint pointers

* During work breaks, wrap paintbrushes or rollers in newspaper or plastic wrap.
* Overnight, put paintbrushes in water or brush cleaner as directed on the can.
* Suspend the brush so it is not resting on its bristles and the water doesn't reach the metal parts. Ideally, make a hole in the handle, push a skewer through this, and balance it on the rim of a jam jar half filled with water. Shake and wipe before beginning painting the next day.
* At the end of a job, wipe the paint off on newspaper and wash with water or cleaner. Rinse in warm water and leave to dry.
* Wash latex paint off a roller until the water runs clear. Wrap roller in newspaper, and squeeze out any excess water. If painting with an oil-based paint, wipe the surplus on newspaper, and use the appropriate cleaner. Leave to dry.
* Neglected brushes can be revived. Place the bristles in a pan with a little boiled vinegar, and simmer for 30 minutes. Wash in a detergent solution, rinse, and shake dry.

girly boudoir

A BEDROOM SHOULD BE A HAVEN OF PEACE AND TRANQUILLITY, WITH NO HARSH OVERHEAD LIGHTING. THE ALL-IMPORTANT COMFORT FACTOR MEANS THAT GOOD, FIRM MATTRESSES AND CRISP COTTON BED LINENS ARE ESSENTIAL.

Escaping to a bedroom haven is a pleasant diversion from the day's drudgeries, preferably in the company of a yummy box of chocolates and a gripping read. My ideal modern-day boudoir is somewhat more pared down than the typical Rococo version, spilling with satin and lace, but nonetheless enticing.

Your boudoir can be as compact or as spacious as your needs and space limitations dictate. Even a tiny room can accommodate a Hollywood bed, which can be appropriately dressed and draped. What is important, however, is how you introduce an element of prettiness. A color scheme based on mint green walls and soft rosy pink details is bright, light, and suitably girly. The bed should be romantic, with a tented harem feel.

Traditionally shaped metal bed frames look good, especially if you paint them in a rosy pink. If the frame is already painted, sand it, apply an undercoat, and finish with two layers of matte eggshell for durability.

ingredients

* Walls in mint green latex flat
* Nylon mosquito nets
* Simple folding and slatted table
* Pleated paper lampshade
* Pretty printed cotton bed linens
* Simple metal beds painted in soft pink eggshell
* A box of chocolate violet creams and a good book

tip

PAINT PREP
* Before painting, move any small items, including furniture, lamps, curtains, and books, to another room.
* Place any larger pieces in the center of the room, and cover with a drop cloth. Protect any flooring.
* Remove the handles from the doors and window frames.
* Next, prepare all the surfaces that are to be painted, in the correct sequence: ceilings first, then walls, and lastly wood- and metalwork. Do not skimp on this part. You'd be amazed at how long a pro takes to prepare a room for painting and how short a time it takes to execute the paint job itself.
* See page 18 for more details on decorating preparation.

Give the same color treatment to pleated paper lampshades with a couple of coats of latex flat. The paintbrush can also be applied to small bedside tables—a simple folding slatted wooden table normally found in garden departments looks stylish. Apply one coat of all-purpose primer, and finish with two coats of eggshell. Use white, as too much pink detail might overdo the effect.

Flowing and diaphanous drapes made from filmy nylon can be hung from the ceiling on a circular frame. These are both easy to find and inexpensive. To hang the frame, screw a hook into the ceiling, ideally into a joist so that if a toddler or a cat, wishing to practice its climbing skills, should pull down the net, the frame will stay attached to the ceiling. The net can also serve a practical purpose, in humid regions, as a mosquito deterrent.

Make the bed with pretty girly cotton duvet covers or sheets patterned with a retro pink and green floral print. To achieve the maximum princess feel, layer with as many pillows and cushions as you desire.

make the difference

> 66 Dress your bed in fresh new linens for a simple bedroom update. 99

sleep tight

The simplest way to change the mood in a bedroom without a complete redecorating job is with a change of sheets, blankets, and covers. But remember to choose patterns that look okay with the rest of your bedroom; the look will jar if you're a minimalist girl and your bed is bursting with flowery swirls, for example.

In summer, white cotton or linen sheets and a light creamy wool or cotton blanket provide the perfect cover in an air-conditioned bedroom. The bottom sheet should be the best you can afford—ideally 100 percent cotton percale with a 200 (or more) thread count. If you hanker after pure linen, buy it old from markets, as it will be cheaper and often superior quality.

Fresh blue-and-white seaside cotton stripes teamed with pale indigo sheets are also good summer bedding ideas and not hard to source.

As winter draws in, it's time to think about tucking up with more blankets and cozy textures. Try old-fashioned brushed cotton flannel sheets in pajama-striped pinks or blues— grown-ups appreciate them as much as little people.

Blankets are back, so go hunting at markets and auctions or ask elderly aunties if they have any stashed away in their linen closets. Natural fibers last longer when it comes to blankets, too. Take a large mortgage out if you crave cashmere, slightly less for mixing it with lambswool; or go for a pure wool cellular version.

Keep snug with the addition of a comforter, which is as varied as its usurper the duvet—duck feather or down, goose down, or real eiderdown, which costs, literally, thousands. A secondhand store or market might yield an old eiderdown in a pretty faded paisley or floral print. Freshen it by airing it outside in the sunshine.

wash

10 WAYS TO MAKE A PAMPERING BATHROOM

1 Prioritize. Make a room plan on graph paper (see page 16). Discuss the costs with a plumber before going ahead; a more efficient hot-water heater might be a wiser investment than that state-of-the-art shower you have your heart set on.

2 Cotton textures and great scents. Buy white cotton towels, bath mats and robes (all machine washable) along with good soaps and lotions.

3 Wipe-down surfaces. Stone, wood, cork, and rubber are all good. Avoid carpeting and natural sisal, as they rot. Use bathmats to soak up water on floorboards. Choose matte surfaces for floor tiles, or you will slip.

4 Cotton roller and Roman shades, café curtains and opaque glass all give privacy.

5 Heat. Install a towel-warming rail; in a very small space, consider a slim, tall, wall-mounted design. Infloor heating is a really good choice for the bathroom, particularly under heat-retaining ceramic surfaces.

6 A thermostatic valve on a shower allows you to control the temperature of the water safely. The best have an automatic shut-off, which prevents scalding if the cold-water supply is interrupted.

7 Waterproof paint textures repel moisture. Use latex semigloss or a quick-drying moisture-resistant eggshell finish.

8 Think eco. A quick shower uses much less water than the $3\frac{1}{2}$ gallons (25 liters) used in the average bath. Remember, though, that a 10-minute shower uses more water than a bath. Consider solar power to heat water, particularly if you live in a sunny climate.

9 If you can't afford to start again, update what you have; give floorboards a fresh coat of paint and replace tired-looking bath tiles with new ones. Streamline your bathing space by boxing in fixtures with tongue-and-groove paneling.

10 If you need a new shower, you might consider the kind on a flexible tube. Some can be fixed at different heights, so are particularly good for children—or if you just want to wash your feet. When held free of the wall, the showerhead makes easy work of washing the shower stall or bathtub.

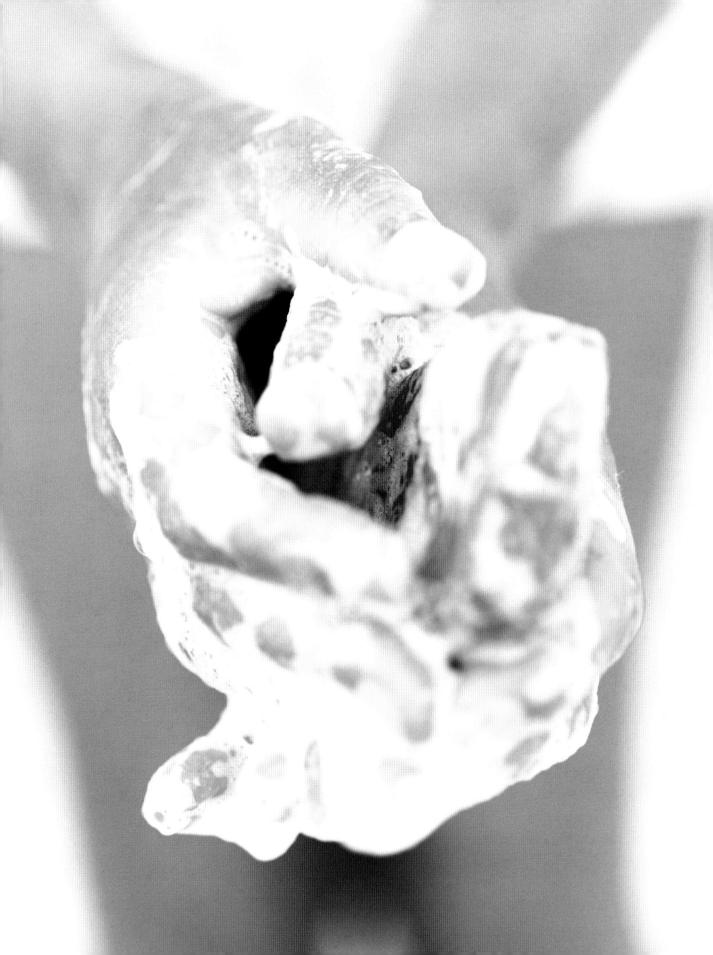

simple style

CREATE A SNUG WHITE BATHROOM WITH TONGUE-AND-GROOVE PANELING.

Boxing in bathtubs, sinks, and unsightly plumbing is a useful way to streamline an old-fashioned bathroom. It can be achieved using various devices such as tiling or wood paneling. Interiors guru Katrin Cargill has gone one step further in her London townhouse. This girl's heart lies in the mountains, so she has decorated her entire bathroom in rustic style using lengths of tongue-and-groove paneling to line the walls and to box in all the pipework. All of the materials used were quite cheap, and the costs were further reduced by using simple moldings for the baseboards and shelf edges.

Durable white eggshell paint gives the walls a good matte look as well as a tough, water-resistant coating.

The traditional-look clawfoot cast-iron bathtub is just the right sort of roly-poly shape to gently envelop the bottom and back during a long, hot soak. Stern beauty editors might disapprove of this practice (too drying on the skin), but most of us would admit that the sheer body-reviving sensation of warmth and weightlessness is worth it after a long working day.

On the subject of cast-iron bathtubs, it should be noted that they are extremely weighty, and you should check up on the strength of your floor before installing one. If you need to remove an old beaten-up one, it's much easier to break it up on site with a sledgehammer. I know because we did this at home and so saved the bother of hiring some muscle to heave it down the stairs.

ingredients

* Walls clad in pine tongue-and-groove paneling painted in white eggshell
* Wooden floorboards sanded and painted in white floor paint
* Freestanding clawfoot bathtub
* Telephone-style chrome showerhead and faucet
* Pretty gathered café curtain in blue-and-white dot-print cotton
* Fluffy cotton bathmat to soak up any drips

tip

DEALING WITH PAINT SPILLS

* Move fast—if possible, deal with any spills the moment they happen.
* Remove latex paint splashes from floors with a damp rag while the paint is still wet. Once dried, spots are difficult to budge, but should respond to rubbing with fine steel wool dipped in soapy water. Follow the grain of the wood, use very little water, rinse well, and rub dry.
* Remove latex paint stains on fabric with a sponge dipped in cold water. If the fabric permits, leave the stained material to soak in cold water, then wash in the normal way.
* Sponge oil-based paint stains with mineral spirits or turpentine.
* Spilled paint on a wood or stone floor can be removed if dealt with immediately. Use a brush, spoon, or newspaper to quickly get up as much as you can. Then throw dry sand or garden earth onto the stain, and scrub hard with a broom. On a stone floor, rub in all directions. On a wooden floor, brush the way of the grain only. Sweep up the sand or earth. If any stain remains, wash with washing soda dissolved in hot water.
* Paint splashes on windows can be removed by rubbing with a cloth dipped in hot vinegar.

hot water and white towels

TEXTURE AND WARMTH ARE ESSENTIALS IN THE SIMPLE BATHROOM.

If you're planning a new bathroom and money is tight, the golden rule is to aim for simplicity. Resist the urge for a hi-tech, all-spraying-and-steaming shower system or the beautiful but pricey hand-baked Moroccan tiles, as seen in the latest interiors magazine. The good news is that it's possible to buy basic bathroom fixtures at a home store without forsaking style. Thus, body and soul can be soothed and cleansed without going into the red.

I followed this route when furnishing our simple family bathroom. With five family members, plus the occasional lodger, I knew that our utmost priority was hot water, and lots of it, at any time, so I purchased a mega-flow hot-water heater, which was installed downstairs in the utility room. Although a significant part of the budget was taken

ingredients

* Walls painted in white latex semigloss paint
* Walls part-tiled in white square ceramic tiles
* Wooden floorboards sanded and painted in white floor paint
* Bathtub boxed in with tongue-and-groove paneling
* Telephone-style hand-held showerhead with integrated faucet
* Chair covered in white terry cloth (see page 122)
* White cotton roman shade
* Worn wooden bathtub caddy and wire soap dish
* Fluffy white cotton towels

tip

TILE TIPS
* Nail battens to the wall at right angles to form the framework in which to start tiling. Check that the battens are level with a spirit level.
* Spread adhesive over 1 sq. yd. (1 sq. m.) and put the first tile in position.
* Place tiles in horizontal rows, pressing into position and checking that they are level.
* Insert spacers between each tile (matchsticks will do).
* Remove battens and spacers when all the whole tiles have been laid and the adhesive is set.
* Cut and fit any remaining tiles. Hold the tile to be cut back to front in the space to be fitted. Mark with a pencil. Turn the tile over, then score with a tile cutter and a steel ruler. Put a matchstick at both edges of the tile under the scored line. Press on both edges to snap it.
* Apply grout between the tiles with a sponge when the adhesive is set.
* Run a wet finger along the grout lines for a smooth finish. Clean the surface with a cloth when grout is dry.

up by this beast, I had enough left over to buy a white bathtub, sink, and toilet. A word of warning though: if you're going for economy models, avoid those with decorations, which look very tacky. Choose a simple, honest-looking design.

Luke, our Polish carpenter, made a cradle to support the enameled steel bathtub and then boxed it in with tongue-and-groove pine paneling. We then used 6-in. (15cm) square basic white tiles around the tub—also from the same source—and painted the walls in white latex semigloss, which has a good waterproof texture.

From a salvage yard, I bought a utilitarian thirties' chrome towel-warming rail; old ones are easy to find here in England, where they've been standard fixtures for ages. The towels are also bargains—half the normal price because they're seconds—but a pulled thread here or there is barely noticeable.

A chair cover made from a towel is a simple and comfortable bathroom detail. (See page 122 for a simple pull-on chair cover idea.) Underfoot there are wooden floorboards painted with white floor paint. A cotton bathmat is usually laid to soak up drips, which would otherwise sneak through the cracks in the boards.

simple shower

MAKE A SIMPLE WALK-IN SHOWER USING THE SKILLS OF A GOOD BUILDER, WATERPROOF TEXTURES, AND GLEAMING WHITE TILES.

Showering should be as invigorating and refreshing as diving through romping surf. However, the all-too-usual musty shower stalls that one comes across in cheap apartment conversions or public swimming pools induce such feelings of squeamishness that, frankly, I'd rather go unwashed. With its hefty membership fees (my treat to myself), this was not the case at the snazzy city sports club where I'd escape my motherly duties for the regenerating torrents of hot water in sleek glass cubicles.

Could I have my own walk-in wet room at home? Our indefatigable builder claimed he was installing them all the time for his mega-buck clients. But could we do it on a shoestring? "Leave it to me," was his reply.

So we ripped out the old fixtures from a 10 x 4 ft. (3 x 1.25m) bathroom and erected a 5-ft. (1.5m)- long floor-to-ceiling stud partition wall to make a walk-in shower stall. To the left of the entrance is a towel-warming rail and sink, and to the right, a built-in closet to conceal the shower pipes and to store towels. The partition wall is hung with hooks, behind which lies the door-free shower area.

The bathroom walls and floor were lined with waterproof marine ply and the floor was raised to make a gentle slope for the water to drain away. We used simple white tiles on the walls, which were waterproofed up to a height of 8 in. (20cm) using three layers of waterproof resin. The shower pipes were concealed in the cupboard behind the shower. The shower itself is equipped with a thermostatic valve, which enables the user to set the temperature of the water and prevent those unexpected scalding or freezing moments—an important factor when children are showering.

On the floor we laid matte mosaic tiles, which are non-slip. These come attached to an adhesive sheet, sold by the square foot (30cm square), which makes them quick to lay. Both the floor and wall tiles were grouted in an off-white waterproof grout (white discolors quickly and looks dirty against white tiles).

Where we live, a showerhead is likely to get clogged up with lime deposits. If you have this problem, here's what to do: Unscrew the showerhead and place it in a saucepan with a mixture of equal parts white vinegar and water. Bring the mixture to the boil, and the deposits should come off.

ingredients

* **Walls** in white ceramic tiles finished with an off-white grout

* **Floor** in white ceramic sheet mosaic tiles, also finished with an off-white grout

* **Thermostatically controlled shower** and simple watering-can style chrome showerhead

* **Simple downlighter**

tip

TILE TROUBLESHOOTING

* Before tiling over, plaster fill cracks and holes in walls, then paint with plaster primer.
* Remove any water- based paints from walls before tiling.
* Remove any wallpaper from walls before tiling.
* Use a flexible tile adhesive when applying tiles to plywood or particle board.
* If tiling over an existing tiled surface, rub it down with sandpaper and wash before starting.

by the seaside

WATERY BLUE HUES ARE GREAT FOR A FRESH LOOK IN THE BATHROOM.

The notion of dressing a bathroom in watery hues is a cliché, but blue is such a deliciously evocative color—whether it conjures up a gray-blue sea, a cool blue lake or a lone swimmer in the pool scything through early morning turquoise water—that it is convincing nonetheless. If you're a water baby at heart, liquid blues can be splashed around the bathroom to make the perfect washroom retreat. To make sure you get the right shade of blue, buy one or more of the sample jars now available, and try the colors on the wall.

I used a rich cobalt blue latex flat from a widely available paint range to bring a shot of fresh, by-the-seaside color into our Spanish bathroom. It is a color that lifts the mood and is a good antidote to dark winter skies (yes, even the Andaluçian south occasionally suffers from the leaden gray skies typically associated with England). Picking out the window frames and mirror in white eggshell adds useful, contrasting color, which stops the blue look from becoming overpowering.

A Victorian towel rail rescued from my grandmother's house is painted in a sea green shade of eggshell paint for more seaside-inspired detail.

ingredients

* **❋** Walls painted in cobalt blue latex flat
* **❋** Woodwork and mirror painted in white eggshell
* **❋** Towel rail painted in sea green eggshell
* **❋** Fluffy white cotton towels
* **❋** Spotlight above sink (check with an electrician before installing)
* **❋** Wall-mounted sink with visible drain looks utilitarian and is space saving

A window flung open to the sunny outdoors creates a lovely feeling of light and spaciousness. Fine for some, but if you're an urban apartment-dweller with limited space in the bathroom, it is worth using light-reflecting, white tiles and choosing your accessories cleverly. A small wall-mounted sink or one designed to fit into an awkward corner would be a good choice, as would a cantilevered toilet, which not only makes the floor area look larger but also simplifies cleaning the floor.

tip BASIC NOTES FOR FIXING THINGS

You can put up anything from a light framed picture to a heavy cabinet with the right fittings. Here are some key tips:

✎ Nails—choose the correct one for the job in hand. Round or oval for wood, steel for masonry, galvanized and nonferrous for use outside.

✎ In hard wood, it's easier to insert a nail once a small hole has been made; use a bradawl to make one, then hammer in the nail at a slight angle.

✎ A piece of cardboard or paper can be used to hold a small nail or tack in place while it's being hammered.

✎ Use masonry nails for fixing light loads such as small framed pictures.

✎ Screws—most are made of mild steel, but there are also brass, aluminum and stainless steel ones for outdoors.

✎ Screwed joints are much stronger than nailed ones.

✎ For small screws, use a bradawl to make a hole; otherwise a drill is usually needed.

✎ Drive in the screw with a screwdriver that fits the head exactly.

✎ Use anchors and screws for large mirrors, shelves, and cabinets.

✎ If the wall is not solid—for example, if it's made of wallboard separated by studs—make sure to insert the fixings in a stud.

make the
difference

"Simple ideas for storing bathroom kit make a wash space both functional and good looking."

neat and tidy

Inventive storage ideas will enable you to keep your bathroom streamlined and tidy. Here are my favorite storage solutions.

✳ Make a roomy drawstring laundry bag in unbleached muslin, and sew on appliqué flowers (see the appliqué cushion on page 128 for inspiration). Hang it on the back of the bathroom door, and fill with your dirty clothes until wash day.

✳ If you prefer colored towels to white ones, choose colors that coordinate well. Subdued greens and blues are cool and fresh looking. You could revive graying white towels by dyeing them your favorite color (see page 142).

✳ To enjoy a long soak in the bath, get yourself a bathtub caddy. These handy little trays, which fit over the two edges of the tub, hold soap, washcloth, pumice stone—whatever items you need. You can choose a metal caddy or, for a more natural look, one made of teak.

✳ A peg rail is useful for face towels, washcloths, and any other hangable objects. Use simple painted wood ones, or something in chrome, if you want to look more modern.

✳ A stacking cart, such as a plastic vegetable rack, is a multi-purpose idea and great for storing bathtime accessories.

✳ Plain white ceramic tumblers are smart and simple holders for toothbrushes.

✳ Use blue-and-white enameled tin plates from a camping shop as utilitarian and stylish soap dishes.

✳ Recycle pretty bottles. Olive oil bottles are rather lovely to decant your favorite cologne into.

✳ Simple open shelving is useful for storing kit above the sink.

✳ A lockable wall-mounted cabinet will prevent little ones from experimenting with the family's medical supplies.

work

10 WAYS TO MAKE A HARDWORKING HOME

1 Room with a view. Work by a window to make the most of natural light and keep in touch with your surroundings.

2 Task lighting. Hinged desk lamps are inexpensive and practical work lighting. White or retro-style metal ones are the best looking.

3 Utility room for washing, drying, and ironing. Even if it's a poky space, you'll find it pleasanter to close the door on laundry than have it draped around the house.

4 Open shelves for books and boxes to file household papers, clippings, and research material. You can never have too many.

5 What to do with trash? Recycle plastic, metal, and paper at your local depot. For the "what, where, and how" of recycling in your community, check the Internet or your local Yellow Pages.

6 Cast your eye around junkyards and secondhand shops for old work tables, office chairs, and filing cabinets, which you can update with a lick of paint.

7 If closet space is limited, buy plastic crates that stack on top of each other to store D. I. Y. tools and any painting kit. Don't hang on to dregs of paint, as it goes off quickly. Take any almost-empty cans to your local refuse dump.

8 Decorate with whites and neutrals—peaceful and undemanding colors to work in.

9 Eco-office. Recycle old computer equipment, save envelopes for reuse, and use recycled papers for writing on.

10 Eco-utility. Cut down on harsh household chemicals such as bleach. Half a cup of baking power in the machine with a liquid detergent revives whites in a wash. Use vinegar and water to clean everything from tiles to windows. Save newspapers for covering surfaces when doing home-improvement and polishing shoes.

on the shelf

SIMPLE FURNITURE AND PRACTICAL STORAGE ARE ESSENTIAL FOR A CALM AND ORDERED WORK SPACE, PROVIDING THE PERFECT BLANK CANVAS FOR INSPIRATIONAL MOOD BOARDS.

To maximize the use of available space, employ a good carpenter to build shelves as tall as your ceiling height allows. Since you will have to pay for labor and materials, this will turn out to be more expensive than buying freestanding shelving, but size and shape will be tailored to suit your particular needs.

I would suggest using particleboard to cut down on the cost of materials. Cheaper than solid wood, it is made up of small chips of softwood bound with glue, which is squeezed between rollers to make smooth sheets of the required thickness. Plus points: it has an even texture and is resistant to warping. Downsides: it bows if support is inadequate, the cut edges may be uneven, and special screws are needed for fixing.

An alcove equipped with shelves in this manner is a brilliant space saver. Snugly supported with a central spine, these shelves are 2 ft. 6 in. (75cm) wide, 10 in. (25cm) deep, and 14 in. (35cm) tall to accommodate most magazines and box files. Tip: For small books like paperbacks, fit a false back to the bookcase to make a shallower shelf.

For efficiency, stack the tallest books at the bottom, together with boxes of paints, work folders, and work bags. Keep a sturdy stepladder on hand for reaching the higher shelves.

ingredients

✱ Walls painted in white latex flat

✱ Particleboard shelves painted in white eggshell

✱ Secondhand table painted in white eggshell

✱ White cardboard ready-to-assemble file boxes

✱ Cork tile bulletin board (see page 116)

✱ Table lamp with cream parchment shade

tip

HOW TO PAINT FLOORBOARDS

✱ For the smoothest finish, sand the floorboards with an industrial sander (see page 60).

✱ Vacuum and mop the floorboards, and leave them to dry.

✱ Apply one coat of primer/undercoat with a paintbrush and leave to dry for time stated on can.

✱ Floor paint is particularly sticky, so it is wise to wear rubber gloves while applying it with a paintbrush.

✱ Apply the first coat of floor paint following the length of the boards. Leave to dry for up to 12 hours or the time stated on can.

✱ Apply a second coat. Some floor paint takes several days to become really hard, so it is wise to keep the space empty until then.

✱ Floor paint is pretty hard-wearing but it does scratch. Consider a repaint after a year or so, but remember that with each repaint the flat, smooth look will not be so apparent.

✱ Keep the painted floorboards clean with a mop, hot water, and detergent.

✱ If boards have been painted in white floor paint, break the eco-rules every now and then, and wash with water and bleach to bring back the whiteness.

✱ If there isn't the budget for an industrial sander you can simply clean the boards and hand sand, before applying layers of undercoat and paint. The finish will not be as even, however, and so less pleasing aesthetically, and the boards will be harder to keep clean.

make the difference

basic utility storage

Built-in closets are an investment as you will need to employ a carpenter. Costs can be reduced by using cheaper materials, such as interior plywood or MDF (medium-density fiberboard) to make the frames and doors.

Plan your space carefully, and make a sketch with accurate measurements (see pages 16–17 for an example). Think about the size of the objects that you want to store, including those things that are used less frequently as well as those items that you need to use every day.

If plumbing is involved, consider the siting of the main drain; it will be an important factor if it is a distance from your planned site.

> 66Built-in closets are the simplest and most space-saving method of storing the clutter of domestic life. 99

CLOSED Doors: Tongue-and-groove wooden doors have been primed and undercoated, then finished with two coats of oil-based eggshell paint. Simple handles have been painted white to keep the wall of storage uninterrupted. Baskets: Traditional rustic baskets are both utilitarian and textural—what better way to carry a bundle of washing out to dry?

OPEN Shelves: Layers of shelves provide storage for towels and linens. Slatted shelves help the air to circulate and keep linens dry. Solid shelves store an iron and cleaning materials. Cupboards: A narrow cupboard houses an ironing board, foldaway clothes airer, and bathroom tissue rolls; a wide one serves as a hideaway for the washing machine, with space above for a basket of laundry.

so easy

DRESS UP A WORK NICHE WITH PRETTY PAPER AND PRINTS.

Even if your nest is spatially challenged, and you have sacrificed the spare room for a child, a roomer, or a partner who is easier to live with if they have their own hideaway, find a niche, even if it's tucked in the corner, for your work and creative musings. Make it pretty and personal, and you're bound to feel more inclined to get down to business.

In this example, pale powder blue wallpaper in an old-fashioned floral contrasts with a junk-purchase desk, contemporary floor lamp and painted frames with black-and-white photos to create a fresh and eclectic work space.

If a small area can't contain the tools of your trade, earmark shelves or closets elsewhere in the house (I have borrowed what was the old built-in linen closet at the top of the house to house my collection of fabric lengths and remnants). If this isn't a possibility, buy cheap stacking boxes or drawers in white plastic or cardboard to keep things neat and tidy.

Similarly, a small desk will cope with a laptop or basic sewing machine, say; but if you need more space for laying things out, consider trestle tables with separate painted wooden tops that can be folded away if you need to use the space for something more pressing. There's nothing wrong with the floor for cutting out dress patterns or laying out presentations.

ingredients

* Walls papered in powder blue floral wallpaper
* Painted frames with ribbon detail (see page 138)
* Junk table
* Chair covered in pull-on slipcover (see page 122)
* Floor lamp for pools of soft light
* Flexible work task lighting

tip

REMEDIES FOR WALLPAPER PROBLEMS

TEARS: Cheap papers tear and are difficult to hang, so use medium-price ones. Perhaps paper only one wall if money is tight. The wallpaper will also tear if it is left to soak too long.

UNSTICKING: Damp walls and too little paste can stop paper from sticking. Press edges of paper with a cloth or seam roller to make sure they stick.

MISMATCHING PATTERN: If the pattern doesn't match, it is usually due to irregular stretching because the strips have been soaked for varying times.

BUBBLES: Lumpy paste and insufficient brushing out will cause bubbles. If wet, lift the paper and smooth out. If dry, cut a cross at the center of the bubble and stick down the flaps.

work hard

A SIMPLE UTILITY SPACE MAKES LIGHT OF DOMESTIC CHORES.

I wouldn't give up my pantry (a proper walk-in one with shelving for all our food) but I dispensed with a second bathroom to make a utility room. I find it efficient and calming on the mind to be able to do the laundry and ironing in a separate room—a necessity at home, where there are always vast piles of washing to process.

It isn't a big space—about 10 x 5 ft. (3 x 1.5m)—but it's just large enough to iron and listen to the radio in peace; and to accommodate a counter and sink with space below for a washing machine and laundry basket.

I'd strongly recommend a ceramic farm sink. They come in various permutations, but the deep ones are very useful for washing things like oven trays, muddy dogs, paint buckets, and hand wash-only stuff. They must sit on some kind of support—either a chrome base with legs or a cabinet that can be used to store cleaning materials.

If you arm yourself with a spirit level, it's not too irksome to put up a simple shelf with brackets (see page 58). Paint in white eggshell for a tough, wipeable finish.

Similarly a wood countertop should also be sanded and sealed with two coats of a clear eco-friendly wood sealant. Use fold-up clothes airers if you don't have a tumble dryer—the old-fashioned wood ones that accordion-fold into a flat shape are much more sturdy than most plastic or metal ones. Best of all, if you have a garden and it's clement weather, dry everything outside on a clothesline.

ingredients

* **Walls painted in white latex semigloss**
* **Wall below shelf painted in chalkboard paint**
* **Countertop in block board**
* **Ceramic farm sink on built-in particleboard cabinet**
* **Open shelving for storage**
* **Storage pots made from recycled plastic (see page 120)**
* **Fold-up laundry basket**
* **Pretty apron for looking glam while doing the chores**

tip

HOW TO UNBLOCK A SINK

Household debris, kitchen waste, and hair are the most likely reasons for a sink to be blocked. Try to deal with it yourself before calling in an expensive plumber. You'll need a rubber plunger. Block the overflow vent, if any, with a rag, and fill the sink with enough water to cover the head of the plunger. Slide the plunger over the drain opening and pump it up and down a dozen times. Pull off the plunger to break the seal with the sink. Repeat this until the water empties. If this doesn't work, remove the trap, or open the clean-out plug (first placing a bucket underneath), and use a piece of wire to clear the pipes on either end of the trap. If the waste doesn't drain, the blockage is beyond the trap. Rent a plumber's snake to investigate further, but at this stage, you're likely to need a plumber.

study area

MAKE A SIMPLE FOLDAWAY DESK FOR WORK AND STUDY.

If you're proficient with a saw and electric drill, why not make your own foldaway work desk? It can easily be cleared and closed when it's time to play or chill out.

Start by screwing a piece of 2 x 4-in. (5 x 10cm) framing lumber, 48 in. (120cm) long, securely to the wall, with the top edge about 30 in. (75cm) above the floor. For the desk top, use a piece of 1-in. (2.5cm)-thick particleboard or solid wood measuring 48 x 24 in. (120 x 160cm). For the legs, use two pieces of 2 x 4-in. (5 x 10cm) framing lumber, the same length as the distance from the top edge of the fixed batten to the floor. Using two $1^1/_2$ x 2-in. (4 x 5cm) hinges, screw the legs to one long side of the desk top, near the corners, with the 4-in. (10cm) sides parallel to the long side. Position one leg 2 in. (5cm) farther back than the other, so that the two legs will lie side by side when the desk is folded away. Congratulate yourself that you have gotten this far, and take a break.

Now, with the help of a friend (more hands make lighter work), screw three 4 x 2-in. (10 x 5cm) hinges to the back edges of the underside of the desk top. Your friend can help line up the desk top with the batten while you screw the other side of the hinges in place.

Now you have the perfect surface on which to study or work. If like me, you are an expert in displacement activity, leave the brain work a little while longer, and give your handiwork the finishing touches by sanding, priming, undercoating, and finally painting the desk with two top coats of eggshell.

ingredients

* Walls painted in white and red stripes
* D.I.Y. foldaway desk in wood and particleboard
* Sofa bed covered in pink cotton corduroy
* Patchwork printed cotton and canvas cushions (see page 128)
* Floorboards painted in white floor paint

FLOORBOARD FLAWS

SQUEAKING OR LOOSE BOARDS: Tighten the boards so that they don't move by screwing the boards onto the joists. For extra firmness, hammer in extra nails, and sink the heads below the surface with a nail set.

GAPS BETWEEN BOARDS: This happens when there is shrinkage due to heating or splintering due to rot. Replace any really damaged boards with new ones. Small gaps can be lived with, and a few large ones can be filled with strips of wood made level with the surface, but any floor riddled with gaps would benefit from being covered with underlayment. If you have the patience and money, the whole floor could, of course, be lifted and relaid.

garden

10 WAYS TO MAKE AN OUTDOOR ROOM

 Plan: Plan your outside space as you would an interior room, with sketches, colours, textures, and list of plants that you like.

Short cuts: Paint bamboo canes and make your own teepees for quick-growing climbers, like clematis and climbing roses. Buy herbs, such as rosemary, lavender, and box in bulk—much cheaper—to plant as pretty hedges.

Dig. Get your soil turned and composted and import some new topsoil, if necessary. It's worth paying for some muscle for the jobs.

If you've got a steeply sloping lawn or seriously infertile soil, but like spending time outdoors, consider adding a deck. Make it large enough to accommodate a table and a few chairs and containers for growing some gorgeous plants.

 As long as you punch holes for drainage, plants can be grown in almost anything: plastic bowls, old sinks, wooden tubs, metal buckets. The key is to feed and water plants regularly. My favorites are leggy lilac or white agapanthus, which both thrive when packed together in terracotta pots.

Cover ugly surfaces with a lick of paint. "In" colors: matte pea green and organic sludgy blues and grays. "Out" colors: harsh wood stains in electric blue and white gloss finishes.

Inspiration: my heroes are David Hicks, for his pragmatic garden design ; Gertrude Jekyll, for her practical advice; Joy Larkcom, for her salad growing tips and for great advice.

For a soft, springy lawn, spread with inches of topsoil, then tread down and reseed. To maintain good drainage, spike every fall with a fork, and brush in topsoil and sand. The growth of lawn grasses combined with regular mowing will keep weeds under control.

Natural textures: old bricks laid in herringbone patterns to edge borders or make pathways; terracotta placed in a checkerboard pattern; a line of old flagstones; gravel pathways; sturdy canvas and thick cotton.

 Look in secondhand shops for garden furniture; there are often simple benches and folding chairs. Garden tables can be improvised using salvaged doors and a couple of trestles. Then there are basic but perfectly acceptable all-in-one picnic benches with seating—very inexpensive and more stylish once painted.

dig it

GROW GOOD THINGS IN YOUR GARDEN, INCLUDING VEGETABLES FROM ORGANIC SEED AND LOCAL VARIETIES.

Dig a vegetable plot in the garden. Or, if you're an apartment dweller, see if a busy friend with a big yard will let you cultivate vegetables for both of you in part of it. For the best results, dig in plenty of good soil mix or—even better—your own compost. This is the key to rich, nourishing soil, from which you will be able to grow succulent, flavorsome produce.

You can buy containers for compost heaps, or you can build your own, using bricks or concrete blocks or planks of fencing. Be sure to include some holes for ventilation.

Place sticks or other coarse material at the bottom to let the air in. Use leaves, vegetable waste, wood shavings, eggshells, lawn cuttings, and tea bags, and build in layers. Water the heap, and cover it with earth and a lid to keep the heat in and speed the rotting process. If you then build a second compost head alongside the first, you can soon start taking well-rotted compost from the first.

Border the vegetable patch with utilitarian paths, made from planks of wood (see right) old bricks, broken shells, pebbles, gravel, or old bricks. Or you could try pretty edgings using herbs like mint, chives, and parsley, or hazel sticks bent to make scalloped edges. I recycled Victorian terracotta ridged edgings from the front garden to make simple boundaries for my new vegetable and flower plot—which will, I hope, start to show the fruits of our winter labors later on this year. I am growing beans and tomatoes up tepees, together with rows of onions, lettuces, potatoes, zucchini, spinach, and arugula.

ingredients

* Good home-made compost
* Good things to grow, especially organic seeds
* Canes to train beans and tomatoes
* A large sun hat

tip

HOW TO MAKE A TEPEE

* Not only do they add height in the garden but tepees built from canes are perfect for training up beans, tomatoes, sweetpeas, and other cottage garden climbers.
* Bamboo canes are available in garden centers and some hardware stores. They come in various lengths; I'd go for one about 7 ft. (2.2m) long; this will make a tepee approximately 6 ft. (1.8m) tall, with another 1 ft. (30cm) to be pushed into the soil as a support.
* To construct, take six sticks, bunch them together, and bind at 2 in. (5cm) below the top with lengths of raffia to make a 2-in. (5cm)-wide band.
* Splay the sticks out tepee-style, and push into the ground.
* Three or four tepees in a row look good; or position one at each corner of a vegetable patch.
* Paint the canes in a garden green latex paint to look stylish.
* Don't regard a tepee as a permanent fixture, as it will rot naturally after a few years.
* Consider other materials, such as lengths of cut hazel for organic-looking and woody tepees.

potted garden

PUNCH A HOLE IN THE BOTTOM OF ALMOST ANY CONTAINER; THEN FILL IT WITH SOIL, PLANT IT UP, WATER, FEED, AND WATCH THE GARDEN BLOOMS GROW.

The paved terrace outside Mandy Bonnell's kitchen door (also see her retreat on page 108) becomes a blaze of color when the contents of her bucket containers are in full bloom. For someone who had "bulbs growing upside down four years ago" Miss Bonnell has come a long way with her gardening self-education, supplied by plant guides and the pearls of TV gardening gurus. Now she knows how to pierce the bottom of a bucket with a bradawl, throw in stones or brick pieces for drainage, and fill with a good potting mixture to make the perfect growing medium. In spring she has tulips, fritillaries, and narcissi (all planted the right way up), which are supplanted later by nicotiana, poppies, and good things to eat such as basil and tomatoes (San Marzano, a plum variety). For year-round greenery there is a huge pompom privet—"my extravagance, but much cheaper than box." Mandy clips it twice a year, in May and August, to keep it in shape.

ingredients

* Walls painted in off-white latex flat (redone yearly)

* Fifties pale blue and white buckets from secondhand shops and flea markets

* Pompom privet grown in an old metal trashcan

* Simple white folding metal table and wooden chairs

tip

HOW TO PAINT POTS

Machine-made terracotta pots can look a bit too perfect, so it is a good idea to give them a bit of textural color for a more weathered look. I make a wash of latex flat (watering it down with an equal amount of water for a thin consistency) in whatever color suits the garden. I usually use white for our cool patio in Spain and a soft bean green for our London back garden. Before painting, simply clean the pot and wipe off any dirt. Either apply one coat of thinned latex flat for a washed-out look or add another coat if you want more defined color. Leave to dry for at least one hour before planting.

color in the garden

MAKE THE DIFFERENCE IN THE GARDEN WITH A FRESH LICK OF PAINT.

The little garden toolshed was in a sorry state, gently rotting at the end of the garden, until it was given a facelift with pale powder blue eggshell on the windows and door and a soft bean green shade in a couple of coats of oil-based undercoat.

The great thing about paint is that you can use it to add style and color to your outside space, even if it's a garden in its infancy or the most basic balcony. Use it to embellish elements such as furniture or trellis, to unify patched runs of fencing, to revive a worn-out shed.

Your choice of color depends somewhat on where you live. If it's a temperate region, choose an understated color that will blend in with your surroundings, such as a subdued blue or green. White looks fresh and perky for details and is the traditional favorite for a picket fence. Avoid bright colors, such as yellow, orange, or lime green, unless you live in a hot climate.

Tough specialist outdoor finishes can be costly, but there are ways to cheat and save money, such as using interior latex flat on walls—if you don't mind doing a yearly repaint. The soft green color I so desired for my fence came from an expensive range of outdoor stains, but I took a shortcut by matching the pigment by computer at a paint store and had it added to an oil-based undercoat that looks great and is tough and weather resistant.

Important: When painting metal furniture, use a rust-proofing undercoat and then an oil-based undercoat with a top coat or eggshell. Gloss paint gives too much of the shine factor.

ingredients

* Shed walls painted in soft bean green oil-based undercoat

* Shed windows painted in powder blue eggshell

smart shed ideas

* Paint the interior walls white for a light and bright seaside look; or choose a soft garden green or blue.
* Fit your shed with shelves, and paint them in the same color. Use them to store all your garden kit.
* Fix simple hooks to the walls, so that you can hang up everything from your garden apron to a net bag of spring bulbs.
* Stick to bare floorboards, which can be given a good scrub; they are the most practical floor surface.
* Collect wooden crates from a garden center to use for storage. You could even paint them.
* Keep a couple of chaises longues and a foldaway table in your shed. Spread with a tablecloth and decorate with lanterns or hurricane lamps for a romantic retreat or summer picnic.

pint- sized urban retreat

A FORMAL GARDEN SHAPE WITH INFORMAL PLANTING IDEAS

Print maker Mandy Bonnell's tranquil garden, a stone's throw from thundering city traffic, was an overgrown mound when she started work on it just three and a half years ago.

The plan: to create a formal shape—echoing the proportions of her Georgian townhouse—with an informal array of cottage garden plants. Working with elbow grease, shovels, and a wheelbarrow, Mandy rearranged the existing gravel to make box-edged paths which wrap around a central bed bordered with flagstones and "little lottie" dwarf lavenders.

Filling up her tiny garden is Mandy's passion, and, since she is without a car, she depends on mail-order bulbs and seeds from cottage garden plant specialists.

On the north-facing back wall, there are shade-loving specimens: an early flowering Montana clematis, climbing hydrangea, ferns, and hostas. On the side walls, Mandy cultivates phlox, deep red sunflowers, aquilegias, dahlias (cut down and protected under flower pots over winter), campanula, standard roses, and a quince tree. The central bed is packed with leggy alliums, a gorgeous "raspberry ripple" iris and gladioli (a much-maligned plant in the upper echelons of garden design).

ingredients

* Gravel and flagstone paths
* Old brick walls
* Beds edged in box and dwarf lavender
* An array of cottage garden blooms
* Shade-loving plants for a north-facing wall
* White painted wood and metal bench

tip

HOW TO LAY A BRICK OR GRAVEL PATH

* Work out a plan before you start.
* It's worth employing a building contractor (check that he is experienced in outdoor works) or a garden designer (probably much more expensive) for this sort of heavy work.
* Patios and paths need a firm base if they are not to sink into the ground.
* The ground should be leveled as much as possible beforehand.
* A layer of ballast should be shoveled on, then a layer of cement to make a hard level surface on which to lay bricks, stone, or gravel.
* Drainage is important, so the surface should slope gently toward a drain.
* Old weathered bricks look great in herringbone and other brick- wall tiled patterns. Don't have flush pointing, as it looks very ugly; the brick layer won't like it, but ask for it to be below the level of the bricks. Fill the remaining space with silver sand.
* Old flagstones are beautiful, but they are expensive.
* Consider gravel—the cheapest option and available in various colors, sizes, and textures.

cool white patio

MAKE A ROOM OUTSIDE IN SUMMER

At the start of the summer vacation in Spain, I put on my spattered pinstripe painting shirt and pink cowboy scarf to repaint the graying exterior walls in our patio garden. Up here in the hills, after the heavy winter rains, it is a necessary task. The traditional way is to use whitewash; but since it's a time consuming business mixing it all up, I'm afraid that I head for the local paint store to buy cans of latex flat to do the job, quickly and cheaply. Hell, I want to get out there in the sun! One coat is enough to make it all look fresh.

Out come the garden tables; having been stored inside, they don't need attending to. Next I rig up my outdoor lighting system of lanterns strung along the wall. By day we sit under a blue and white striped cotton awning, which is stretched across the yard. At night it's rolled back to reveal the stars, as we feast on goodies from the BBQ and summer salads.

Try this idiot-proof idea for roast vegetables: Slice chunks (about ½ in. [1cm] thick) zucchini, eggplant, onions, tomatoes, bell peppers, and garlic gloves. Put in a shallow roasting dish. Sprinkle with 2–3 tablespoons olive oil and a few sprigs of thyme and rosemary. Cook at 300°F (150°C) for 45 minutes or so, turning occasionally, until soft and crisp. Feast on sardines grilled on the fire, plates of roast vegetables, and something ice-cold to drink.

ingredients

* Walls painted in white latex flat
* Table painted in eggshell
* Cushions and cloth in cotton fabrics
* Glass holders for candles
* Metal lanterns

tip

SHADY BUSINESS

Make an awning to give cooling shade to an outdoor patio by stretching an extra-large piece of canvas from one wall or fence to another.

* Look for extra-wide canvas. This can be found at specialist hardware stores. The wider the canvas, the better, so you don't have to sew too many pieces together to get the spread.

* Fix as many hooks as necessary, all at an equal distance, along each wall or fence. Depending on the boundary wall or fence, aim to place the hooks at a height of approximately 7½–8 ft. (2.3–2.4m).

* Hem any raw edges on the canvas, making sure it is large enough to give the spread needed.

* Stitch pairs of 4-in. (10cm)-long pieces of cotton tape along the length of the canvas to match up with the hooks on the wall, and use these to fix the awning in place.

PART 3

20 things to make and do

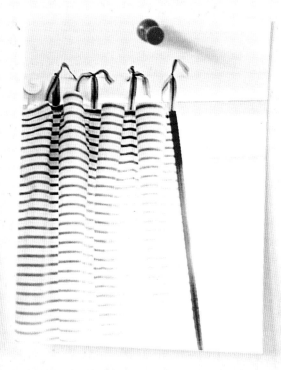

potato print

THE HUMBLE POTATO IS A MOST USEFUL TOOL FOR CREATING A SIMPLE POLKA-DOT PRINT. SIMPLY LOAD A CUT SPUD WITH PAINT TO MAKE A PRETTY SPOT DESIGN.

If you want random spots, simply apply them at will. For a more regular pattern, mark out equidistant rows, using a pencil and long measuring tape. Someone to hold the tape will make the process quicker.

STEP 1. Simply cut the roundest potato you have in half. Mold it into shape with a knife if it's not quite as circular as you want—don't worry about making it perfect; the charm of this technique is its handmade, irregular quality.

STEP 2. Pour the paint—latex is good—into a paint kettle or bowl, and dip the potato in. Don't overload it, or the paint shape will splodge and run when applied to the wall.

STEP 3. Stamp the potato cut firmly on the wall to make the spot shape; repeat if not defined enough.

STEP 4. Allow to dry for about an hour; then step back and admire your handiwork.

“Soft pistachio green painted polka dots give a sweet, yet contemporary wall finish. ”

cork tile bulletin board

PIN UP IMAGES TO INSPIRE YOUR CREATIVE FLOW. PAINT THE BOARD IN A PALE POWDER
BLUE OR SIMILAR SUBTLE SHADE TO LET OTHER COLORS SING THROUGH.

When gluing the tiles to the wall surface, make sure you
press the cork tiles down very firmly, as they can lift away
from the wall. If the wall is slightly uneven or the tiles are
going to be painted, I recommend using the tile supplier's
own brand of water-based glue.

STEP 1. Mark out your desired dimensions of the bulletin
board onto your wall surface. My bulletin board is seven tiles
high and five tiles wide. If you have an awkward space to fill,
don't worry—just cut the tiles to size.

STEP 2. It is most important that the wall surface be
clean; wash it down with de-greaser, and leave to dry before
applying the tiles.

STEP 3. Check your measurements carefully, then glue
the cork tiles to the wall surface, following the
manufacturer's instructions.

STEP 4. Leave the tiles for approximately 24 hours to
allow the glue to dry thoroughly. Once the glue is dry, paint
the tiles with two or three coats of latex paint.

materials

**To make one bulletin board approximately
84 x 60 in. (213cm x 152cm):**

✱ 35 cork tiles, 12 in. (30cm) square

✱ Tape measure

✱ Pencil

✱ Water-based glue

✱ Latex paint

✱ Paintbrush

painted wall stripes

WANT MORE COLOR IN YOUR LIFE? MAKE A BOLD STATEMENT WITH WIDE PINK AND WHITE PAINTED STRIPES OR WHATEVER COLORS YOU LIKE.

materials

* **✳ Newspaper or dropcloth**
* **✳ Extending tape measure**
* **✳ Low-tack masking tape**
* **✳ Pencil**
* **✳ Large paintbrush**
* **✳ Paint tray or kettle**
* **✳ Latex paint in two contrasting colors ("A" and "B")**

When painting in the stripes, use one coat of paint if you want to see the brush marks; if you prefer a solid color, add a second coat.

STEP 1. Thoroughly prepare the surface to be painted (see pages 13 and 73). Make sure the wall is free from any dirt and dust. Mask off all electrical outlets, baseboards, floor edges, and where the wall meets the ceiling, using low-tack masking tape. Put down the newspaper or drop cloth. Paint the wall that is to be decorated with a base coat, using one color ("A"). Allow paint to dry.

STEP 2. Measure the width of the freshly painted wall, and mark the center with a pencil. Working from the center point of the wall, measure 6 in. (15cm) to either side of this point, and mark. This will form the central contrasting stripe in "B".

STEP 3. Mask off this first stripe from floor to ceiling with the low-tack masking tape, placing the tape on the outer edges of the marked stripe. Check that the vertical lines are straight using the spirit level.

STEP 4. Continue masking off 12-in. (30cm)- wide vertical stripes across the rest of the wall, but remember to place the masking tape for every "B" stripe on the outside edge (therefore just inside the border of the "A" stripes). When the entire wall is masked off, paint in all the "B" stripes as shown. Allow paint to dry; then carefully peel off the masking tape to reveal the design.

1 & 2. Measure center of wall, and mark central stripe in pencil.

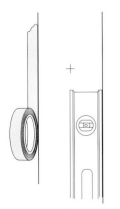

3. Mask off central stripe on outside edges, and check with spirit level.

4. Mask off stripes across entire wall. Paint alternate stripes in contrasting color. Allow to dry then peel away tape.

painted plastic pots

GET INTO ECO MODE AND TRANSFORM PLASTIC WATER BOTTLES, CREAM CARTONS, AND YOGURT POTS INTO SIMPLE STORAGE CONTAINERS.

Paint the insides of the pots, too, to make them look more finished; a paler or darker shade of the outside colour looks very effective.

STEP 1. Empty and rinse out the plastic bottles, making sure they are thoroughly clean and dry.

STEP 2. Cut off the tops of the bottles to give the required size and shape.

STEP 3. Place the bottles on the newspaper. Paint the cut-down bottles with two or three coats of latex paint, allowing the paint to dry between each coat, until the plastic is perfectly covered.

materials

* Selection of plastic bottles and pots
* Sharp scissors or utility knife
* Newspaper
* Paintbrush
* Latex paint

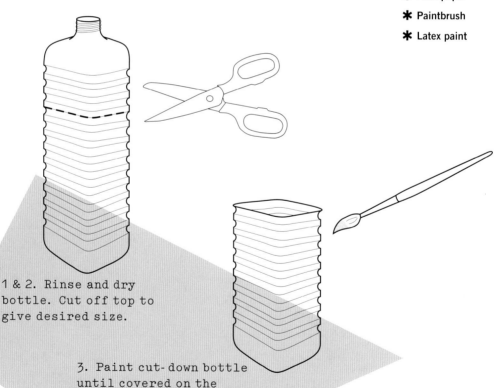

1 & 2. Rinse and dry bottle. Cut off top to give desired size.

3. Paint cut-down bottle until covered on the inside (if desired) and then on the outside.

simple chair cover

DRESS UP PLAIN KITCHEN CHAIRS WITH PRETTY PULL-ON GINGHAM COVERS, CUT FROM A SINGLE PIECE OF FABRIC AND TAILORED TO FIT.

Budget-priced but pretty and washable, gingham is a good choice for a crisp and modern look.

STEP 1. Measure the chair to be covered. Use newspaper to make a pattern. Trace the lines of chair front, back, and the chair seat to create a pattern for the chair cover from a single piece of fabric, adding seam/hem allowances on each side. Include a drop from the seat, again plus generous seam/hem allowances.

STEP 2. Lay the material out flat, pin the pattern to it and make the cuts in the material as shown on the diagram, so that the chair cover can be fitted at the seat corners. Do not cut the sides until you are sure that they are in the right place.

STEP 3. Stitch the back and front together, with right sides facing down to the point where the chair back meets the chair seat. Leave the rest free.

STEP 4. Turn front/back right side out. At each inner corner, cut diagonally to the depth of the hem allowance. Hem all the raw edges around the chair skirt. Fit cover over your chair and relax.

materials

* Fabric, such as lightweight gingham
* Tape measure
* Sharp scissors
* Sewing thread
* Dressmaker's pins

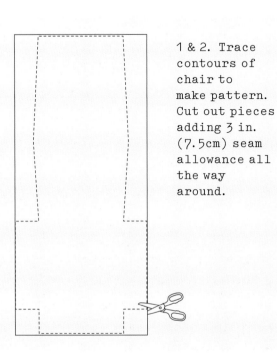

1 & 2. Trace contours of chair to make pattern. Cut out pieces adding 3 in. (7.5cm) seam allowance all the way around.

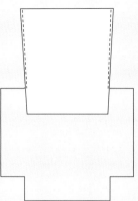

3. Sew the front and back to the point where they meet the seat.

4. Fit over the chair and hem to the length required.

painted secondhand table

WITH GOOD PREPARATION AND A COUPLE OF COATS OF PAINT, EVEN THE SCRUFFIEST PIECE OF FURNITURE CAN BE GIVEN A SMART NEW LOOK.

Use an oil-based eggshell paint to make the surface of the piece of furniture more resilient to stains and spills.

STEP 1. Place the piece of furniture on top of some sheets of newspaper or a drop cloth. Sand down the wood using medium-grain sandpaper, working along the grain, rather than across it. Wipe down the table with a damp cloth to make sure it is free from any dirt or dust.

STEP 2. Paint the entire table with one coat of combined undercoat/primer. Start with table top and move down the legs, following the grain of the wood. Allow to dry. If the wood grain still shows through, apply another coat.

STEP 3. When the undercoat is dry, apply two coats of oil-based eggshell paint following the same painting sequence for a good, even finish.

"I find that my best secondhand buys are both functional and simple in shape."

curtained dressing table

STORE YOUR JEWELS AND TRINKETS ON A PRETTY PAINTED DRESSING TABLE HUNG WITH A LIGHTWEIGHT, FILMY SKIRT.

Using muslin or a similar lightweight fabric for the skirt will let the light through and look exceptionally pretty.

STEP 1. Follow all three steps given in the instructions for the Painted Secondhand Table on page 124.

STEP 2. Measure the perimeter of the front and sides of the table to calculate the amount of fabric you will need. The length of the curtain is up to you. Mark out the measurements of the fabric, allowing $3/8$ in. (1cm) seam allowance all the way around, plus $1^1/4$ in. (3cm) hem allowance along the top and bottom edges. Cut out the fabric.

STEP 3. Turn and stitch a $3/8$-in. (1cm) hem along all sides of the fabric. Turn and stitch a $1^1/4$-in. (3cm) hem along the top edge of the curtain to make a casing through which the tape can be threaded. Turn and stitch a $1^1/4$-in. (3cm) hem along the bottom edge.

STEP 4. Attach the ribbon to the top of the curtain just below the casing by sewing along the outside edges. The ribbon should be about $3/4$ in. (2cm) from the top of the curtain.

STEP 5. Thread the tape through the casing of the curtain, and fix it in place with a thumbtack at the end of each tape (assuming the table is not a priceless Chippendale).

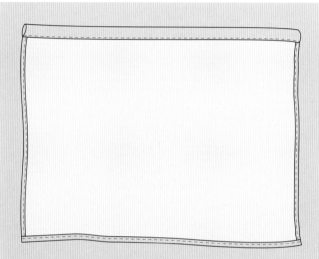

1, 2, & 3. Paint the table. Measure and cut out fabric. Sew $3/8$- in. (1cm) hems along all four sides. Sew $1^1/4$- in. (3cm) casing along the top for tape to be threaded through.

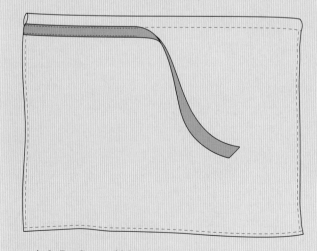

4 & 5. Sew ribbon to top edge. Thread tape through casing. Fix curtain in place around table.

materials

* Small wooden table with an open front
* Newspaper or drop cloth
* Medium-grit sandpaper
* Undercoat/primer
* Large paintbrush
* White latex paint
* Tape measure
* Lightweight fabric, such as muslin, for curtain
* Ribbon, approx 1 in. (2.5cm) wide
* Cotton tape, approx $3/4$ in. (2cm)
* Thumbtacks

groovy appliqué cushion

NOT SURE WHAT TO DO ON A WET AFTERNOON? CUT OUT PRETTY, HIPPIE-STYLE FLORALS FROM PRINTED COTTON TO MAKE GROOVY FLOWER-POWER CUSHIONS.

STEP 1.   From the solid-colored fabric, cut two squares the size of the pillow form adding 2 in. (5cm) to one side and adding 1 in. (2.5cm) seam allowance all the way around. Turn and stitch a 1-in. (2.5cm) hem on one short side of both pieces.

STEP 2.   Draw a flower shape on cardboard or stiff paper. Use as a template to cut out flower shapes from fabric remnants. Leaving the edges raw, pin the cut-out flowers to the right side of the cushion cover pieces, placing them randomly. Hand sew, using neat running stitches in appropriately colored thread.

STEP 3.   Place the two cover pieces together with right sides facing and raw edges matching. Pin or baste together. Stitch a 1-in. (2.5cm) seam around the three unhemmed sides.

STEP 4.   Cut eight lengths of the cord, tape, or ribbon, approximately 8 in. (20cm) long. On each tie, fold one end back neatly; stitch ties in pairs to both sides of the cover opening at equal intervals. When all eight ties are in place, turn the cover right side out. Insert the pillow form and fasten the ties with bows.

materials

* ✱ Solid-color cotton fabric for cushion cover
* ✱ Remnants of patterned fabrics for appliqué
* ✱ Cardboard or stiff paper
* ✱ Dressmaker's pins
* ✱ Sharp scissors
* ✱ Cord, linen tape, or ribbon for ties
* ✱ Pillow form

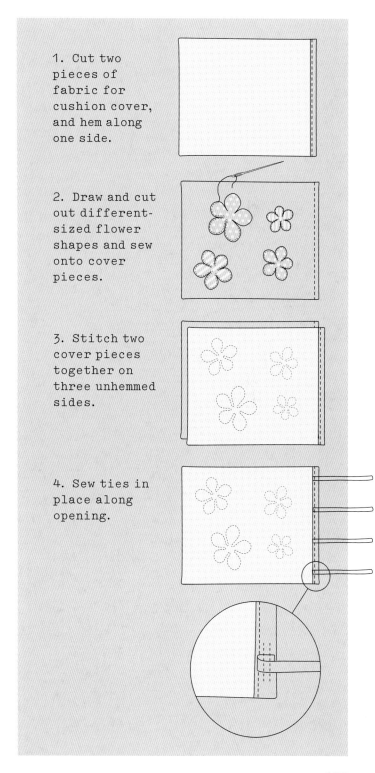

1. Cut two pieces of fabric for cushion cover, and hem along one side.

2. Draw and cut out different-sized flower shapes and sew onto cover pieces.

3. Stitch two cover pieces together on three unhemmed sides.

4. Sew ties in place along opening.

ruffle- edge apron

FOR ANOTHER LOOK, MAKE THE APRON FROM UNBLEACHED MUSLIN AND TRIM IT WITH A RUFFLE OF PRETTY FLORAL OR POLKA-DOT PRINT COTTON.

STEP 1.   Enlarge pattern pieces as indicated. Cut out leaving 1 in. (2.5cm) seam allowance.

STEP 2.   Pin, baste, and stitch length of rickrack to shaped edge of main piece (A) approximately $\frac{5}{8}$ in. (1.5cm) from the edge.

STEP 3.   Stitch two short ends of ruffle pieces (B) together. Press the seam open. Turn under a $\frac{3}{8}$ in. (1cm) hem on remaining short ends. Pin, baste and stitch. Repeat on one long edge. Sew two parallel lines of long machine stitch (or running stitch), $\frac{3}{8}$ and $\frac{5}{8}$ in. (1cm and 1.5cm) from other long edge. Gather it up to fit shaped edge of main piece. Secure gathering threads around pins.

STEP 4.   With right sides facing, align the gathered edge of the ruffle with the shaped edge of main piece. Pin and baste, then stitch between the gathering lines. Remove visible gathering thread. Press seam allowances toward main piece.

STEP 5.   Turn under $\frac{3}{8}$ in. (1cm) on all edges of ties (C). Pin, baste, and stitch.

STEP 6.   Turn under and press $\frac{3}{8}$ in. (1cm) on all edges of waistband (D). Fold in half, wrong sides facing, and press. Gather top edge of main piece to fit waistband. Pin and baste waistband edges over gathered edge and over ends of ties. Stitch in place.

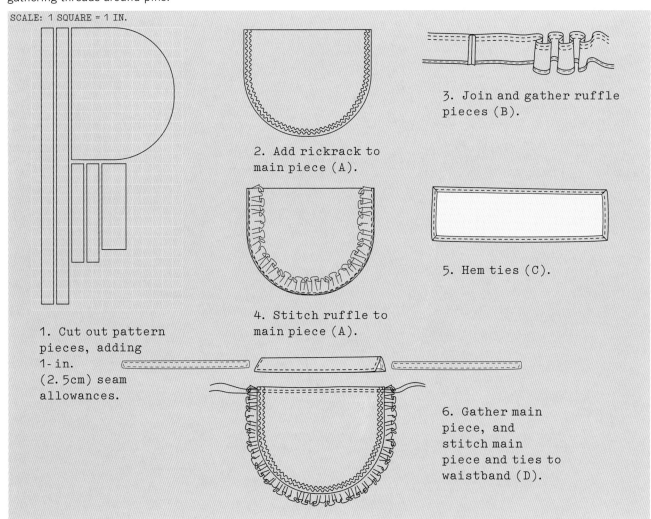

SCALE: 1 SQUARE = 1 IN.

1. Cut out pattern pieces, adding 1- in. (2.5cm) seam allowances.

2. Add rickrack to main piece (A).

3. Join and gather ruffle pieces (B).

4. Stitch ruffle to main piece (A).

5. Hem ties (C).

6. Gather main piece, and stitch main piece and ties to waistband (D).

materials

* Fabric, such as lightweight gingham
* Sewing thread
* Rickrack
* Sharp scissors
* Dressmakers' pins

easy-care slipcover

STICKY FINGER- AND MUDDY PAW-PRINTS? THIS BASIC SLIPCOVER IN STRIPED TICKING CAN BE THROWN IN THE WASHING MACHINE AND WILL COME OUT LOOKING AS GOOD AS NEW.

Try the cover on the chair while you are making it to avoid any surprises. Don't worry about its fitting perfectly—a few bags and sags are part of its charm—but to fit the cover more easily around the arm curves, pin and cut as you go. If the chair that you are covering is perfectly symmetrical, you can leave the cover inside out when fitting it over the chair so any adjustments can be made easily. Slipcovers need to be washable. Make sure the cover is large enough to allow for any shrinkage. If necessary, wash a small sample of the fabric to check for shrinkage.

STEP 1. Remove the cushion from the chair. Make patterns for individual pieces with newspaper, or place fabric directly onto chair following the diagram (see page 135). Spread the fabric out over a large clean table or floor. Cut out sections of roughly the same sizes as the individual parts of the chair. Remember to allow for seams and hems.

STEP 2. Cut a length of fabric for the inside back of the chair, adding 3 in. (7.5cm) all the way around for seams. Using dressmaker's pins, pin the panel to the chair inside back, wrong side out. Cut a length of fabric for the seat, including the drop at the front and adding 3 in. (7.5cm) all the way around for ease/seams. Pin to the chair, wrong side out. Now pin the panel and the seat to the large arm panels. Stitch the skirt to the seat, and attach the horizontal arm verticals. Finally add the outside back.

STEP 3. Trim off all excess fabric to leave a $^3/_4$ in. (2cm) seam allowance all the way around. Remove the pins one by one, and repin the fabric pieces together, making smooth seamlines. Once you have gone over the whole chair, carefully take the cover off. Baste along the pinned edges. Remove the pins and machine stitch. Turn up the hem to the drop length desired, pin and baste. Stitch. Turn the chair cover right side out. Fit the cover on the chair and pin up the hem, then stitch. Now freshen up your ticking cover with a quick press.

STEP 4. For the seat cushion cover, cut out two pieces of fabric the size of the seat cushion, adding $^3/_4$ in. (2cm) all the way around for seams. Cut a side panel from the fabric the same length as the perimeter by the width of the cushion, adding $^3/_4$ in. (2cm) all the way around for seams.

STEP 5. With the right sides facing, pin, then baste the side to the top panel. Stitch $^3/_4$ in. (2cm) from the edges, clipping into the corners. Attach the bottom panel with the right sides facing, leaving an opening at the back for inserting the cushion. Turn right side out. Insert the cushion and hand sew the opening with small, neat hand stitches to close.

materials

* Sturdy fabric, such as ticking
* Newspaper
* Tape measure
* Tailors' chalk
* Sharp scissors
* Dressmaker's pins
* Sewing thread

continued overleaf ☞

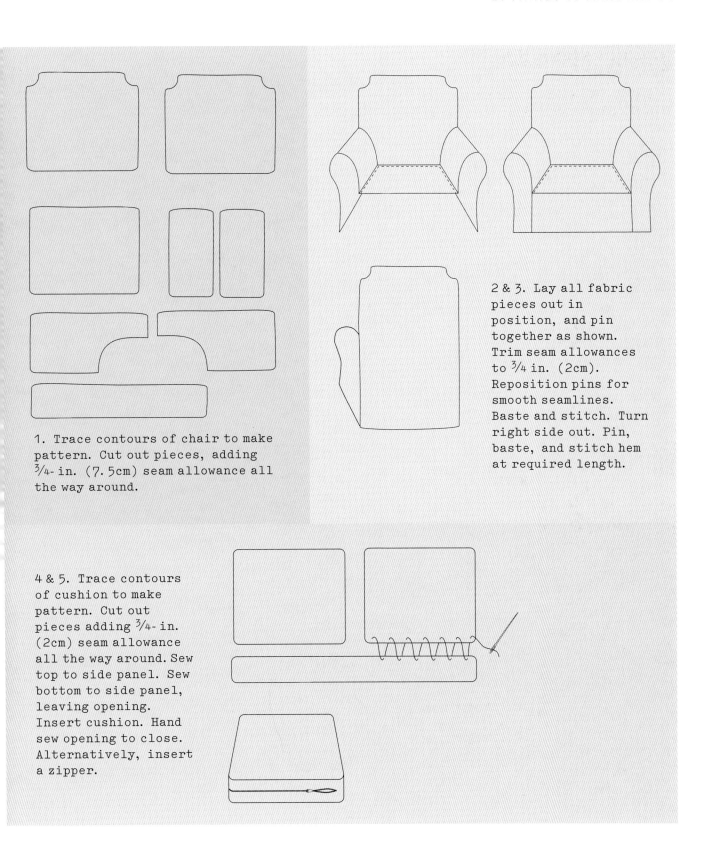

1. Trace contours of chair to make pattern. Cut out pieces, adding ³⁄₄- in. (7.5cm) seam allowance all the way around.

2 & 3. Lay all fabric pieces out in position, and pin together as shown. Trim seam allowances to ³⁄₄ in. (2cm). Reposition pins for smooth seamlines. Baste and stitch. Turn right side out. Pin, baste, and stitch hem at required length.

4 & 5. Trace contours of cushion to make pattern. Cut out pieces adding ³⁄₄- in. (2cm) seam allowance all the way around. Sew top to side panel. Sew bottom to side panel, leaving opening. Insert cushion. Hand sew opening to close. Alternatively, insert a zipper.

painted chest

ALL YOU NEED IS A STEADY HAND TO CREATE THE STRIPE OUTLINE ON THIS SECONDHAND CHEST OF DRAWERS. A STRONG COLOR, LIKE THIS CORNFLOWER BLUE, GIVES CONTRAST.

When masking off the drawer fronts, make sure the masking tape is pressed well down, or the paint will "bleed" and make your lines look blurred and untidy.

STEP 1.   Follow all three steps given in the instructions for the Painted Secondhand Table on page 124. Remove drawers from chest to paint them; otherwise they will become stuck.

STEP 2.   Mask off an even border of approximately 1 in. (2.5cm) around the edges of each drawer front, using low-tack masking tape. Using a small paintbrush, paint in these borders around each drawer front. For a strong color, apply two coats of contrasting paint.

STEP 3.   Once the stripes are painted, slowly and carefully peel off the masking tape to reveal the design. Allow to dry before replacing the drawers in the chest.

> 66 Simple detail such as this contrasting outline is all that is needed to make a perfectly ordinary chest of drawers look really rather stylish. 99

ribbon-hung frames

MOUNT YOUR FAVORITE BLACK AND WHITE PHOTOGRAPHS IN PRETTY PAINTED FRAMES, AND "HANG" THEM WITH RIBBON IN THE HOTTEST COLOR YOU CAN FIND.

The trick here is to nail the ribbon in place first of all and then hang the frames with small nails at appropriate intervals along the lengths of ribbon. Use different-sized frames for an informal look.

STEP 1. Lightly sand down a selection of wooden and plastic secondhand picture frames, using medium-grit sandpaper. Place the frames on sheets of newspaper, and paint each one with an undercoat/primer and then two coats of latex paint, allowing each coat to dry. Once the frames are thoroughly dry, insert your favorite pictures and photographs in the painted frames. If a frame is missing its backing board, cut one from thick cardboard. Attach D-rings to the edges of the frame, and fasten on a piece of picture wire or cord.

STEP 2. Nail a long strip of wide ribbon to the wall where you want the pictures to hang. Cut another length of ribbon about 8 in. (20cm) long, and tie into a knot. Nail the knot over the top end of the strip of ribbon, making sure that the nails cannot be seen.

STEP 3. Beginning at the top of the ribbon, hammer a nail through the ribbon and wall at the correct point for hanging. Hang the first picture, and then repeat for the following pictures, leaving a suitable gap between them, as shown.

materials

* **✳** Selection of picture frames
* **✳** Newspaper
* **✳** Medium-grit sandpaper
* **✳** Undercoat/primer
* **✳** Latex paint
* **✳** Paintbrush
* **✳** Wide ribbon: satin, velvet, or cotton
* **✳** Scissors
* **✳** Small nails
* **✳** Hammer

ribbon-tie pillow sham

THIS BASIC PILLOW SHAM HAS AN ENVELOPE OPENING WITH TIES. CUSTOMIZING THE SHAM WITH RICKRACK AND CONTRASTING RIBBON TIES GIVES IT A SIMPLE AND PRETTY LOOK.

materials

* To make one sham for a standard-size pillow 20 x 26 in. (51 x 66cm):
* Fabric, such as lightweight cotton or linen, at least 55 x 21 in. (140 x 54cm)
* Rickrack, 2^1/$_2$ yd. (2.2m)
* Ribbon, 1^3/$_8$ yd. (1.2m)
* Sewing thread
* Pillow, 20 x 26 in. (51 x 66cm)

STEP 1. For front (A), cut a piece of fabric the size of the pillow, adding ^{3}/$_8$ in. (1cm) seam allowance to each edge. For backs (B and C), cut two pieces of fabric the height (short measurement) of the pillow by two thirds the width, adding ^{3}/$_8$ in. (1cm) seam allowance to each edge.

STEP 2. Cut a length of rickrack the perimeter of front (A). Turning under the ends of the rickrack where they meet, pin, baste, and stitch it just inside the edges of right side of front (A). Lay backs (B and C) right side down, and turn in a double ^{3}/$_8$-in. (1cm) hem on one long side of each. Pin, baste, and stitch. Press. Lay backs (B and C) over the front (A) with right sides facing and raw edges matching, so that the two hemmed edges overlap. Pin or baste together ^{3}/$_8$ in. (1cm) from edges. Stitch.

STEP 3. Turn right side out. Press. For the ties, cut six pieces of ribbon 8 in. (20cm) long. Fold under ^{3}/$_4$ in. (2cm) at one end of each tie, and pin in place, placing ties in pairs on either side of the opening, spacing them evenly. Hand sew each ribbon in place, taking care not to sew through more than one layer of fabric.

STEP 4. Insert pillow into sham, and tie ribbons to enclose.

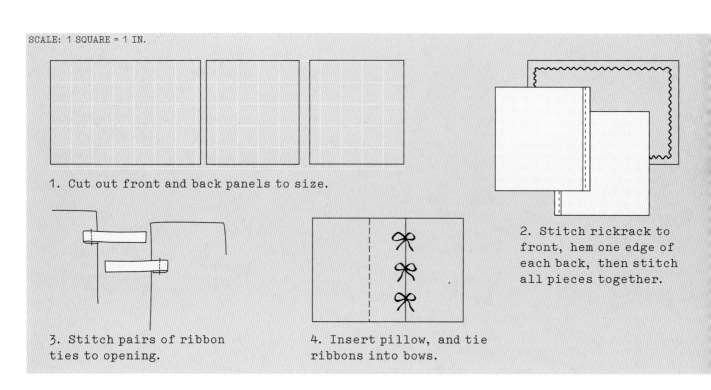

SCALE: 1 SQUARE = 1 IN.

1. Cut out front and back panels to size.

2. Stitch rickrack to front, hem one edge of each back, then stitch all pieces together.

3. Stitch pairs of ribbon ties to opening.

4. Insert pillow, and tie ribbons into bows.

custom-dyed towels

GIVE A NEW LEASE ON LIFE TO TIRED-OUT WHITE TOWELS BY DYEING THEM IN PRETTY SHADES OF PINK AND LAVENDER AND ADDING HANDY HANGING TABS.

For best results when dyeing at home, and when dyeing large items such as towels, use the dye in your washing machine. Always study the package instructions carefully as some recommended dyeing methods of different brands can vary. Do not try to dye too many items at once. Wash the dyed towels separately the first time you use them.

STEP 1. Weigh your towels to calculate how much fabric dye is needed. Check the quantities given on the packet instructions. Dyeing larger amounts of fabric will result in a lighter color. Place your chosen towels in the washing machine, and wash them on a quick-wash cycle to make sure they are perfectly clean before dyeing. Even if towels are new, they must be washed to remove any fabric dressing that will prevent the dye from being taken up. Remove the towels from the machine but leave damp.

STEP 2. Wearing rubber gloves, empty the fabric dye directly into the drum of the washing machine. Do not place the dye in the soap dispenser or in a dispenser ball. Add salt on top of the fabric dye if necessary. Place the damp towels back in the machine. Wash the towels on the recommended wash cycle according to the packet instructions. When the wash cycle has finished, add powder detergent and run through the hottest possible program for the fabric. Remove the newly dyed towels and hang up to dry away from direct heat or sunlight. Wash the dyed towels separately for the first couple of washes to remove any excess dye.

STEP 3. To make the hanging tab, fold a piece of ribbon approximately 6 in. (15cm) long in half, and stitch the open ends together to make a loop. Stitch the sewn ends of the ribbon securely to one corner of the towel.

materials

* **Selection of old towels**
* **Rubber gloves**
* **Machine fabric dye**
* **Salt, if required**
* **Gingham ribbon, approximately 1 in. (2.5cm) wide**

dish towel tablecloth

IF YOU DON'T WANT TO USE DISH TOWELS, STITCH TOGETHER A PATCHWORK OF PLAIDS, STRIPES, AND FLORALS CUT FROM VINTAGE CURTAINS AND CUSHIONS.

materials

* Dish towels or assorted remnants of fabric

* Sewing thread

* Bias strip or ribbon for edging, 2^1/$_4$ in. (6cm) wide

STEP 1. Pin, then baste the dish towels together with ^{3}/$_8$ in. (1cm) seam allowance to achieve the size of tablecloth required. Stitch. Open out the seams, and press flat.

STEP 2. For the edging, cut two strips the length of two opposite sides of the tablecloth plus ^{3}/$_4$ in (2cm). Lay each strip along the edge of the tablecloth, right sides facing and edges matching. Pin, baste, and stitch ^{3}/$_8$ in. (1cm) from the edge. Press seam allowances toward edging.

STEP 3. Bring the edging strip around to the wrong side of the tablecloth, turning under ^{3}/$_8$ in. (1cm). Pin and hand sew in place.

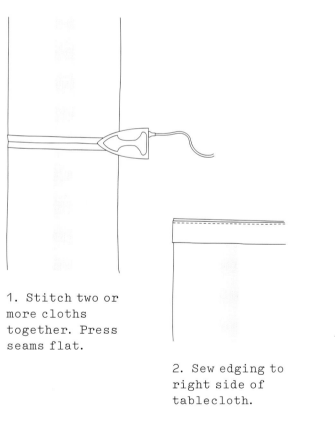

1. Stitch two or more cloths together. Press seams flat.

2. Sew edging to right side of tablecloth.

3. Fold edging and hand sew to wrong side of tablecloth.

ticking curtain

TIE-ON LOOPS ARE THE SIMPLEST WAY TO HANG A BASIC CURTAIN.

STEP 1. Enlarge pattern pieces as indicated. Cut out all the curtain pieces as shown, making sure that the long sides of the curtain tops (A) and (B) are the same measurement as the width of the curtain panels (C) and (D), adding 1 in. (2.5cm) seam allowance all the way around.

STEP 2. With right sides together, align the raw edges of one long side of a curtain top (A) to one short side of a curtain panel (C). Pin and baste together. Stitch 1 in. (2.5cm) in from the edge. Open out the seam and press flat.

STEP 3. Turn under a 1-in. (2.5cm) hem along the top and both sides. Pin and stitch, taking care at the corners.

STEP 4. On the right side, sew a length of ribbon over the seam where the curtain top and main panel join. Attach with parallel lines of stitching as shown.

STEP 5. Turn under a double $^3/_4$-in. (2cm) hem along bottom edge of the curtain. Pin and baste in place. Secure with neat hand stitches.

STEP 6. Repeat all steps for the other curtain.

1. Cut out pieces as shown.

✳ materials

✳ **To make one pair of curtains approximately 130 x 58 in. (325 x 147cm)**

✳ **4$^5/_8$ yd. (5m) striped fabric, such as ticking, 59 in. (150cm) wide**

✳ **Sewing thread**

✳ **7$^1/_4$ yd. (8.3m) ribbon for trim**

✳ **2$^3/_4$ yd. (2.5m) ribbon for ties**

SCALE: 1 SQUARE = 1 IN.

2. Stitch top (A) to panel (C) with 1-in. (2.5cm) seam.

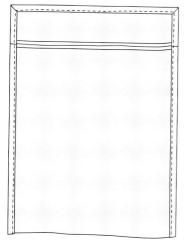

3. Stitch top and side hems.

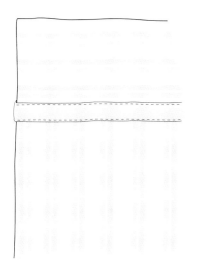

4. Stitch ribbon over seam to disguise join.

5. Stitch hem.

bed linens with ribbon trim

TUCK UP WITH ORIGINAL BED LINEN IDEAS: DYED PLAIN COTTON SHEETS IN HOT PINK TRIMMED WITH STRIKING RIBBONS.

Experiment with other trimmings, such as eyelet lace dyed to your favorite color.

STEP 1. Follow steps 1 and 2 of the Custom-dyed Towels on page 143, taking care to wash the sheet separately at first and rinsing out the machine after dyeing.

STEP 2. Sew your chosen ribbons across the entire width of the sheet at the top edge, stitching along each edge to secure them.

materials

* **Full-size cotton sheet, approximately 81 in. (205cm) wide**
* **Rubber gloves**
* **Machine fabric dye**
* **Salt, if required**
* **$4^5/_8$ yd. (5m) velvet ribbon and $2^3/_8$ yd. (2.5m) grosgrain ribbon**
* **Sewing thread**

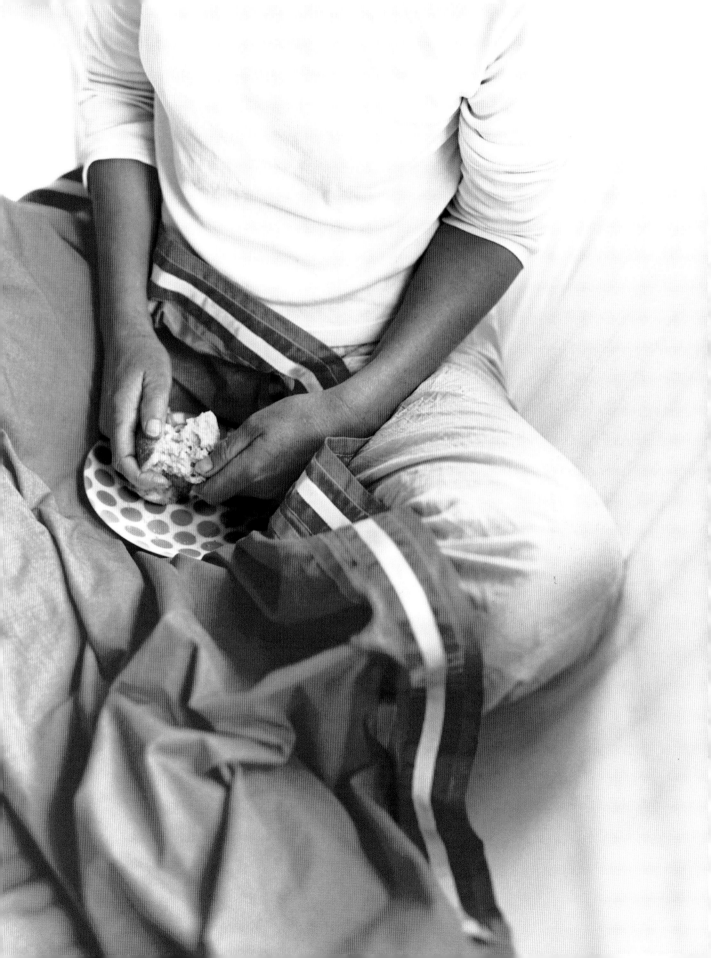

lighthearted lampshade

TREAT YOUR LAMPSHADE AS YOU WOULD A SIMPLE HAT, AND DECORATE IT WITH RIBBONS, BOWS, AND OTHER SARTORIAL TRIMMINGS.

Make sure the lampshade is the right proportion for the base, and also check that the lampshade carrier is the right size.

STEP 1. Place the lampstand on top of newspaper or a drop cloth, and sand, working along the grain. Wipe down the woodwork to remove any dirt or dust. Once dry, paint with two or three coats of latex paint, allowing it to dry between coats.

STEP 2. Cut a strip of fabric twice the circumference of the bottom of the lampshade by 5 in. (12cm) wide. Fold and stitch a 3/8-in. (1cm) hem along the one long edge.

STEP 3. With right sides facing, stitch the short edges of the ruffle together to form a band. Evenly gather the top edge of this band to make a ruffle that snugly fits the bottom edge of the lampshade.

STEP 4. Hand sew the ruffle to the bottom edge of the shade. Cover the top edge of the frill with the ribbon. Pin and hand sew in place to cover any unsightly stitching. For the top edge trim, cut a strip of fabric the length of the circumference of the top of the lampshade and 2 in. (5cm) wide. Fold and press 3/8-in. (1cm) hems along both long edges. With right sides facing, stitch the short edges together to form a band. Hand sew in place around the top edge of the lampshade.

STEP 5. For the bow, cut a piece of fabric 12 x 1 1/2 in. (30 x 4cm). With right sides facing, fold in half and stitch short edges together. Turn right side out. Press. Fold the ends into the middle of the bow, and baste in place. Make another tube measuring 3 x 2 in. (8 x 4cm) in the same way and fold around the middle of the bow to make a knot. Tack into place. Hand sew bow in position on the top edge of the lampshade.

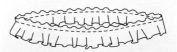

1, 2 & 3. Sand and paint lampstand. Make a ruffle, and gather to fit the bottom edge of the shade.

4. Sew the ruffle to the bottom edge of the shade; cover the sewn edge with ribbon. Sew other fabric tube to top edge of shade.

5. Make fabric bow, and attach to top edge of shade.

materials

- ✳ Wooden lampstand from secondhand shop
- ✳ Newspaper or drop cloth
- ✳ Medium-grit sandpaper
- ✳ White latex paint
- ✳ Large lampshade
- ✳ Fabric, such as cotton gingham
- ✳ Sewing thread
- ✳ Sharp scissors
- ✳ Ribbon
- ✳ Lamp carrier

garden chairs

OLD DIRECTOR'S CHAIRS WITH SHABBY COVERS CAN BE SMARTENED UP WITH CONTRASTING COTTON AND CANVAS TO MAKE HARD-WEARING SUMMER SEATING.

STEP 1. Make sure the chairs are clean and free from dust. Remove any old nails using pliers.

STEP 2. Cut a piece each of the canvas and the cotton the size of the chair seat and back, respectively, plus an extra 4 in. (10cm) for the turn-under and ³/₄ in. (2cm) seam allowance all the way around. With right sides together, stitch the back pieces together on three sides. Turn right side out. Hand sew the opening edges together with small, neat hand stitches. Repeat for the chair seat.

STEP 3. Tack the back and seat panels in place on the wooden chair frame, using five or six tacks for each side of the material.

materials

✱ Director's chair

✱ Pliers

✱ Tape measure

✱ Fabric, such as heavyweight canvas

✱ Fabric, such as lightweight retro-print cotton

✱ Sewing thread

✱ Upholstery tacks

✱ Hammer

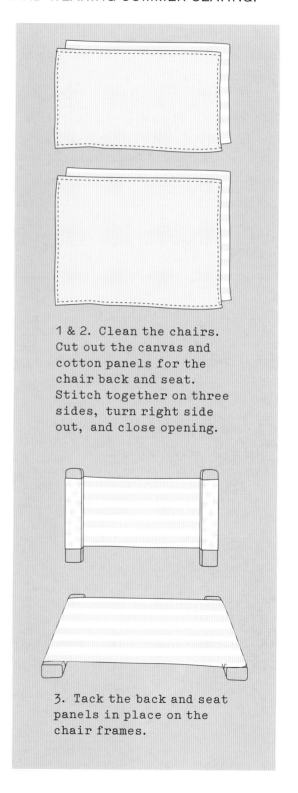

1 & 2. Clean the chairs. Cut out the canvas and cotton panels for the chair back and seat. Stitch together on three sides, turn right side out, and close opening.

3. Tack the back and seat panels in place on the chair frames.

retro bag

TURN OFF THE TV, AND CONVERT A CUSHION COVER INTO A SWEET RETRO BAG IN AS LONG AS IT TAKES TO WATCH A COUPLE OF DVDS.

For a neater finish or contrast colour, add a lining to the bag by making a simple sewn 'bag' by hand stitching in place around the top edge.

STEP 1. For the bag handles, cut two 2-in. (5cm) wide strips from across the top edge of the cover, first removing the zipper, if any.

STEP 2. Cut two pieces of lining fabric the same size as the fabric strips for the bag handles. Place the handle and lining pieces together with right sides facing, and stitch along three sides, leaving one end open. Turn right side out. Fold under the raw edge and close the opening by hand.

STEP 3. For the bag, turn a $^{3}/_{8}$-in. (1cm) double hem to the wrong side all the way around the raw edge of the cushion cover. Pin and stitch.

STEP 4. Pin the handles in place at the top edge of the bag. Attach the handles using reinforced stitching. At each end of the handles, stitch a neat square, then stitch across on both diagonals. Repeat by tracing the previously stitched lines for an extra-secure finish.

materials

* Cushion cover, such as retro print cotton
* Sharp scissors
* Sewing thread
* Small remnants of lining fabric

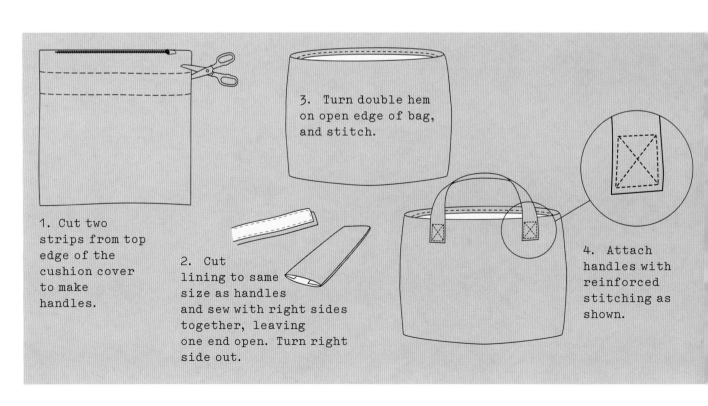

3. Turn double hem on open edge of bag, and stitch.

1. Cut two strips from top edge of the cushion cover to make handles.

2. Cut lining to same size as handles and sew with right sides together, leaving one end open. Turn right side out.

4. Attach handles with reinforced stitching as shown.

sources

PAINT

COLE & SON
www.cole-and-son.com
Striking contemporary and
traditional designs. Printing
since 1873.

DULUX
www.iciduluxpaints.com
A vast collection of paints, including
a heritage range of period colours.

FARROW & BALL
www.farrow-ball.com
A superb range of paints in accurate
heritage colours.

WALLPAPER

COLE & SON
See under Paint for contact details.
Retro and flock designs.

COLEFAX & FOWLER
www.colefax.com
Classic English floral prints.

FARROW & BALL
See under Paint for contact details.
Pretty eighteenth-century inspired florals,
traditionally printed.

OSBOURNE & LITTLE
www.osbourneandlittle.com
Nina Campbell's floral designs and
cotton and upholstery weaves.

PAINT & PAPER LIBRARY
www.paintlibrary.co.uk
Designers and suppliers of inspirational
paints and wallpapers

FABRICS

BEACON HILL
979 Third Avenue
New York NY 10022
Tel: 800 921 5050
A selection of fabrics.

BENNISON FABRICS INC.
76 Greene Street
New York, NY10012
Tel: 212 947 1212
A selection of printed fabrics.

BOUSSAC OF FRANCE
979 Third Avenue
New York NY10022
Tel: 212 421 0534
A selection of fabrics.

BRUNSCHWIG & FILS
979 Third Avenue
New York NY10022
Tel: 212 838 7878
www.brunschwig.com
A selection of fabrics and trimmings.

CALICO CORNERS
203 Gale Lane
Kennet Square PA 19348
Tel: 800 213 6366
Over 100 retail outlets that
discount top-quality fabrics;
also selected seconds.

CLARENCE HOUSE FABRICS LTD.
211 East 58th Street
New York NY10022
Tel: 212 752 7153
www.clarencehousefabrics.com
A selection of fabrics and wallpapers.

COWTAN AND TOUT
979 Third Avenue
New York NY 10022
Tel: 212 647 6900
A selection of fabrics, trimmings,
wallpapers, and accessories.

DESIGNERS GUILD
www.designersguild.com
Fresh stripes, checks and florals. Sheer
organzas, cottons and linen, as well as felt
and wool.

FORTUNY
979 Third Avenue
New York NY 10022
Tel: 212 753 7153
A selection of fabrics.

HINSON
979 Third Avenue
New York NY 10022
Tel: 212 688 5538
A selection of fabrics.

IAN MANKIN
www.ianmankin.com
Ticking in all colours, plus utility
fabrics and good strong canvas
useful for garden chairs.

LAURA ASHLEY INC.
398 Columbus Avenue
New York NY 10024
Tel: 800 463 8075
www.lauraashley-usa.com
A selection of fabrics.

LEE JOFA
979 Third Avenue
New York NY 10022
Tel: 800 453 3563
www.leejofa.com
A selection of fabrics.

MELIN TREGWYNT
www.melintregwynt.co.uk
Checked wool blankets in
blues, greens and yellows.

OPPENHEIM'S
P.O. Box 29
120 East Main Street
North Manchester IN 46962
Tel: 800 461 6728
Country prints, mill remnants,
denim, and chambray.

OSBORNE & LITTLE
Head Office and Showroom
90 Commerce Road
Stamford CT 06902
Tel: 203 359 1500
www.osborneandlittle.com
A selection of fabrics.

PIERRE DEUX
870 Madison Avenue
New York NY 10021
Tel: 212 570 9343
A selection of fabrics.

RANDOLPH & HEIN
101 Henry Adams Street
San Francisco CA 94130
Tel: 415 864 3550
www.randolphhein.com
A selection of fabrics.

ROSE BRAND
75 Nineth Avenue, 4th Floor
New York NY 10011
Tel: 800 223 1624
www.rosebrand.com
Inexpensive muslin, gauze,
canvas, and ticking fabrics.

SCALAMANDRÉ
942 Third Avenue
New York NY 10022
Tel: 212 980 3888
www.scalamandre.com
Fabrics, trimmings, wallpapers, and carpets.

SCHUMACHER INTERNATIONAL LTD.
979 Third Avenue
New York NY 10022
Tel: 800 332 3384
www.fschumacher.com
A selection of fabrics.

STROHEIM & ROMANN
31–11 Thomson Avenue
Long Island City NY 11101
Tel: 718 706 7000
A selection of fabrics.

ZIMMER & ROHDE
979 Third Avenue
New York NY 10022
Tel: 212 758 5357
A selection of fabrics.

ZOFFANY
979 Third Avenue
New York NY 10022
Tel: 212 758 5357
www.zoffany.com
A selection of fabrics.

HOUSEHOLD LINENS

KEEPSAKE QUILTING
Route 25B
PO Box 1618
Center Harbor NH 03226
Tel: 800 865 9458
www.keepsakequilting.com
A good selection of lightweight cottons.

M.K. SWORLS LTD.
P.O. Box 1057
Marlborough MA 01752
Tel: 508 624 6311
Quilts, pillows, and hangings in
the New England Style.

DESIGNERS GUILD
See Fabrics for contact details
Bold coloured and strikingly designed
cotton towels.

IKEA
See Lighting for contact details
Good value cotton towels and
bathmats. Excellent choice for sheets,
pillowcases and duvet covers.

SANTE FE INTERIORS
214 Old Sante Fe Trail
Santa Fe NM 87501
Tel: 800 391 7928
Hand woven rugs, bedspreads,
and textiles made in collaboration
with the Zapotec Indians.

WINDOW TREATMENTS

BLINDS GALORE
Tel: 877 70-BLIND
www.blindsgalore.com
A huge selection of blinds, shades,
and cornices.

COUNTRY CURTAINS
The Red Lion Inn
Main Street
Stockbridge MA 01262
Tel: 800 876 6123
www.countrycurtains.com
A wide selection of fabric and lace
for every style of home.

EVERYTHING FOR WINDOWS
Tel: 800 BLINDS-1
www.everythingforwindows.com
A selection of blinds, shades, custom
drapery, and accessories.

GREAT WINDOWS
12011 Guilford Road
Annapolis Junction MD 20701
Tel: 800 556 6632
www.greatwindows.com
A selection of blinds, shades,
cornices, and other hardware.

J.L. ANTHONY
Distinctive Drapery Hardware
10420 Morrison Road
Dallas TX 75238
Tel: 214 340 0359
www.jlanthony.com
A selection of poles and finials.

RUE DE FRANCE
78 Thames Street
Newport
Rhode Island 02840
Tel: 800 777 0998
www.ruedefrance.com
Country French lace panels and
fabric curtains as well as a selection
of Provençal-style curtains and
home accessories.

SMITH & NOBLE
Tel: 800 248 8888
www.smithandnoble.com
A selection of fabrics and window
treatments.

UMBRA
Tel: 800 387 5122
www.umbra.com
A selection of drapes and rods.

MARY FOX LINTON
distributed by
Intair C.P.S. Design Inc.
180 N.E. 39th Street
Miami FL 33137
Tel: 305 573 8956
A good selection of fabrics for windows.

FURNITURE

ANTIQUES SHOPS USA
www.antiqueshopsusa.com
A useful web directory.

CHATEAU EDGEWATER INC.
P.O. Box 2436
Wilsonville OR 97070
Tel: 503 682 8569
www.edecor.com
Baskets and trunks.

CHERNER CHAIR CO
P.O. Box 2689
Westport CT 06880
Tel: 866 243 7637
www.chernerchair.com
Norman Cherner's classic chair design.

CIRCA 50
Maine Street
Manchester VA
Tel: 877 247 2250
www.circa50.com
Mid-twentieth-century design classics.

COGAN'S ANTIQUES
110 South Palmer Street
Ridgeway SC 29130
Tel: 803 337 3939
www.cogansantiques.com
Antiques center.

CRATE & BARREL
1860 West Jefferson Avenue
Naperville IL 60540
Tel: 800 967 6696
Furniture and accessories.

eBAY
www.ebay.com
Online auction site.

GEORGE SMITH
www.georgesmith.co.uk
Beautiful plump sofas and chairs in
classic shapes.

GO ANTIQUES
www.goantiques.com
A useful web directory.

IKEA
www.ikea.com
Check online for your nearest outlet
Good value contemporary and classic
lamp shades and fittings.

PHILLIPS AUCTIONEERS
3 West 57th Street
New York NY 10019
Tel: 212 940 1200
www.phillips-auctioneers.com
Respected auctioneers.

PICKWICK ANTIQUES
3851 Interstate Court
Montgomery AL 36109
Tel: 334 279 1481
www.pickwickantiques.com
Antiques center.

POOR RICHARD'S RESTORATIONS
Montclair NJ
Tel: 973 783 5333
www.rickford.com
Furniture restorer.

THE POTTERY BARN
2109 Broadway
New York NY 10023
Tel: 212 219 2420
www.potterybarn.com
Mail order:
P.O. Box 7044
San Francisco CA 94120
Tel: 888 799 5176
A selection of furnishings and accessories.

TRI-STATE ANTIQUE CENTER
47 West Pike
Canonsburg PA 15317
Tel: 724 745 9116
tri-stateantiques.com
Antiques center.

RESTORATION HARDWARE
15 Koch Road, Suite J
Corte Madera CA 94925
Tel: 800 762 1005
A selection of furnishings and accessories.

ECO-FRIENDLY

NATURAL COLLECTION
Tel 0870 331 3333
www.naturalcollection.com
Eco-friendly products for all areas
of the home by mail order, clockwork
radios, organic sheets, clothes airers.

GARDEN

DAVID AUSTIN ROSES LTD
www.davidaustinroses.com
Specialists in English roses, climbers
and shrub roses, such as the pink Belle
De Crécy, known for its rich fragrance.
Also good for ground cover roses and
modern shrub roses, including Dapple
Dawn, a soft pink rose with a slight
musk fragrance.

FOOD

SIERRA RICA
Tel 0034 959 127 327
www.sierrarica.com
Organic foods from Andalucia in
Spain, mouth-watering peeled and
cooked chestnuts, vegetable spreads,
sauces and soups.

TABLEWARE

THE CONRAN SHOP
www.conran.co.uk
Plain china, blue and white
Cornishware and simple glasses.

DAVID MELLOR
www.davidmellordesign.com
Contemporary tableware, glasses
and everything for the kitchen.

IKEA
See Lighting for contact details
Unbeatable value basic china,
tumblers and cutlery.

ROBERT WELCH DESIGNS
www.robertwelch.com
Classic, simple cutlery –
my favourite.

WATERFORD WEDGWOOD
www.wedgwood.com
Simple white dinner plates.

index

acknowledgments

This is my fifth book, and, once again, a fabulous team have made it happen. Many, many thanks to: Jenny Zarins, for her beautiful pictures, and her ace assistant Juliette Cockerill; Lawrence Morton for his witty and smart design, Charlotte Kennedy-Cochran Patrick for her creative endeavors; Melanie Williams, Emma Heath, and Tessa Brown for their savvy sewing skills; Kate Storer for more clever illustrations; Alison Cathie, Jane O'Shea, Helen Lewis, and Lisa Pendreigh for their support and dedication to my second title with Quadrille; Clare Conville, my wise agent; Tom, Georgia, and Grace Brown, Daisy Tudor, Esther-Mei Roditi Yeo; Bea the cat and (the late) Pippi the dog for their modeling talents; Clare and John Riley; David and Katrin Cargill, Tessa Brown and Jonny White, and Mandy Bonnell for kindly letting me use their homes for photography; Colefax & Fowler for the wallpaper on page 45 and Farrow & Ball for wallpaper and paint on page 94.